Pacific Northwest Foraging for Beginners

Embracing Nature's Flavors in the Pristine Wilderness – An Essential Field Guide to Wild Edibles

Table of Contents

Introduction

The Pacific Northwest has a temperate climate ideal for producing a variety of edible fruits, nuts, and berries. This makes it a perfect region for foraging enthusiasts. If you're open to researching before venturing out, you can quickly find a bounty of delicious goods. Whether you're only starting or someone with years of experience with foraging, this book aims to enhance your knowledge and skills to help you identify edible plants in the region. It enables you to figure out what's safe to eat and what to avoid.

Have you ever looked at a plant and wondered if it was safe to eat? This book can turn those moments of curiosity into moments of confidence. Begin by exploring your local environment to get started with foraging. Look around in various places – perhaps on your property, near barns and sheds, or even in open fields, provided it's safe. It's fascinating to realize that many of the plants listed in this book grow alongside others that are poisonous, so it is necessary to identify them correctly.

For instance, have you ever been hiking and encountered a plant you couldn't identify? This guide will teach you to recognize edible plants and distinguish them from their toxic counterparts. For example, areas prone to landslides can be particularly tricky. Even if the soil has shifted, toxic plants could still be present and partially buried, posing a hidden danger.

Timing your foraging trips is another critical consideration. Each season offers different treasures. In summer, you might find an abundance of ripe berries and fruits, while winter could reveal a harvest of nuts and mushrooms. Picture yourself walking through a winter forest. The trees are bare, the ground is covered in leaves, and suddenly, you spot a patch of wild mushrooms. Knowing when and where to look is key to a successful foraging adventure.

Considering the impact of weather on your finds is crucial. Food can quickly decay when exposed to heat and light. For example, during the hot summer months, autolysis can cause a significant loss of nutrients in the food you gather. Similarly, exposure to the cold can accelerate decay in winter. Therefore, finding a location protected from the elements and animals is essential.

As you read this book, you'll learn about various plants suited to different habitats and how to safely collect and prepare them, including native plants and those introduced to the Pacific Northwest. Have you ever wandered through a meadow and found a plant you couldn't identify? This book will help you understand whether that plant is a tasty treat or something to avoid.

Whether you're an experienced forager or merely curious about the practice, this guide will help you discover local plants, fungi, and small animals that could make up your next meal. Foraging is not only about finding food. It's about connecting with nature and understanding the environment around you. By learning to identify and harvest wild foods, you can enjoy the natural bounty of the Pacific Northwest while ensuring you respect and preserve the ecosystem. So, grab your basket, do some homework, and head out into the wild to explore the edible wonders waiting for you.

Chapter 1: Getting Started with Foraging in the Pacific Northwest

The Pacific Northwest region is famous for its beautiful natural scenery and abundant resources. It includes the states of Washington, Oregon, northern California, parts of Western Montana, the Canadian provinces of British Colombia, and Southeast Alaska. In this opening chapter, you will learn about the environments you can explore, the region's history, and the ethical considerations to remember while foraging.

Ecosystems of the Pacific Northwest

Rugged Coastlines

The Pacific Northwest has some of the most dramatic coastlines in the world.[1]

The Pacific Northwest has some of the most dramatic coastlines in the world, stretching from Northern California to British Columbia. These rugged shores are, of course, shaped by the powerful Pacific Ocean. You can find abundant marine life and coastal plants perfect for foraging here. Edible seaweeds like nori and kelp grow on rocks, while tidal pools are full of mussels, clams, and oysters.

Dense Forests

As you move inland, lush, dense forests cover much of the Pacific Northwest, especially in places like Washington and Oregon. These forests are filled with tall trees like Douglas fir, western red cedar, and Sitka spruce. Beneath these giants, the forest floor is covered with ferns, mosses, and many mushroom species. You'll find numerous varieties of wild edibles and mushrooms in the area. Besides edible plants and mushrooms, the forest is filled with red huckleberries, salal berries, and various other fruits.

Towering Mountains

The Pacific Northwest has impressive mountain ranges, like the Cascades and the Olympic Mountains in Washington and Oregon. These high peaks create differing climates and habitats home to unique plants and animals. Alpine meadows are full of wildflowers in the spring and summer, offering edible greens and roots, like dandelion, wild onions, and yampah. The mountains have hardy berries like huckleberries and elderberries, which ripen in late summer and fall.

The landscapes of the Pacific Northwest are incredibly rich in natural resources. This richness comes from the region's unique mix of climate, geography, and history. The mild, wet winters and dry summers create perfect conditions for many plants and fungi. The volcanic soil is very fertile, helping plants grow well. The region's history, including events like glaciation and volcanic eruptions, has created numerous habitats. These processes have made the area highly biodiverse, giving foragers many species to discover and enjoy.

The Historical Significance of Foraging

Foraging has a long and rich history, deeply rooted in the traditions of Indigenous cultures, and increasingly embraced in modern times as part of sustainable living practices. This section explores the historical importance of foraging, its role in indigenous cultures, and its popularity in today's world as people seek more sustainable and connected ways of living.

Roots in Indigenous Cultures

Foraging has been fundamental to human survival and culture for thousands of years. Indigenous people of the Pacific Northwest, including the Coast Salish, Makah, and Tlingit, have long relied on the region's abundant natural resources for sustenance. These communities developed extensive knowledge about the local plants, fungi, and marine life, which they used for food, medicine, and materials.

Indigenous foraging practices were deeply connected to the land and the seasons. Knowledge was passed down through generations, teaching the best times to harvest specific plants and how to do so sustainably. For example, they knew to only take what was needed and harvest to allow plants to continue growing and thriving. This deep respect for nature ensured the availability of resources for future generations.

Foraging in Modern Sustainable Living

An interest in foraging has recently increased, driven by a growing awareness of environmental issues and a desire for more sustainable lifestyles. Modern foragers are rediscovering the benefits of wild foods, which are more nutritious and flavorful than their cultivated counterparts.

Foraging today is also seen as a way to reduce the ecological footprint. Gathering food from the wild reduces the reliance on industrial agriculture, often associated with high carbon emissions, pesticides, and habitat destruction. Foraging promotes a more sustainable food system, encouraging people to eat seasonally and locally.

It's a no-brainer that foraging develops a deeper connection with nature. It encourages people to spend time outdoors, learn about their local environment, and develop a greater appreciation for the natural world. This connection can lead to more environmentally conscious behaviors and a stronger commitment to conservation.

A Bridge Between Past and Present

The practice of foraging is a bridge between the past and present, linking people to their ancestors' traditions. Learning about and engaging in foraging is an excellent practice to honor the knowledge and practices of indigenous cultures and contribute to a healthier planet.

The practice of foraging is a bridge between the past and present, linking people to their ancestors' traditions.[3]

Foraging is more than a way to find food. Rooted in the traditions of indigenous peoples and gaining new life in modern sustainable living, foraging connects you to the land.

The Enchanting Nature of the Pacific Northwest

The Pacific Northwest is full of mesmerizing landscapes, incredible natural beauty, and ecological diversity. Stretching from Northern California through Oregon and Washington and into British Columbia, this area has various environments with abundant wild edibles. A temperate climate, fertile soils, and varied topography create ideal conditions for various plant and animal life.

Coastlines

The Pacific Northwest's coastline is the region's highlight, with rocky cliffs, sandy beaches, and tidal pools. The interaction between land and sea creates a unique environment rich in edible resources.

Seaweeds

Nori *(Porphyra),* kelp *(Laminaria),* and bladderwrack *(Fucus vesiculosus)* thrive along the rocky shores. These marine plants are packed with nutrients and can be harvested during low tide.

Shellfish

The tidal pools and estuaries are breeding grounds for shellfish, including mussels, clams, and oysters. An excellent source of protein can be foraged by digging in sandy areas or gathering from rocky outcrops.

Edible Plants

Coastal areas support unique plants like beach greens *(Honckenya peploides)* and sea rockets *(Cakile spp.)*, flavorful additions to salads and other dishes.

Green Forests

The Pacific Northwest is covered with dense, temperate rainforests. Although there are various plant species, the most common trees in these forested areas include Douglas fir *(Pseudotsuga menziesii)*, western red cedar *(Thuja plicata)*, and Sitka spruce *(Picea sitchensis)*.

Berries Available

The cooler temperatures and higher elevations support hardy berry species. Huckleberries *(Vaccinium membranaceum)* and elderberries *(Sambucus spp.)* ripen in late summer and fall, providing a delicious and nutritious harvest. Various edible berries thrive in the forest, especially near water sources. Huckleberries *(Vaccinium spp.)* are abundant here and prized for their sweet-tart flavor. Other berries include blackberries *(Rubus spp.)*, thimbleberries *(Rubus parviflorus)*, and salmonberries *(Rubus spectabilis)*.

Mushrooms

The cool, moist conditions of the forest floor are perfect for mushrooms. Chanterelles *(Cantharellus spp.)*, morels *(Morchella spp.)*, and porcini *(Boletus edulis)* are a few of the most sought-after species. These mushrooms are delicious and have unique textures and flavors to enhance various dishes.

Greens and Herbs

Edible greens and herbs thrive in the shaded, nutrient-rich soils of the forest. Nettles *(Urtica dioica)*, rich in vitamins and minerals, can be harvested in the spring. Dandelion greens *(Taraxacum officinale)* and wild onions *(Allium spp.)* are other examples of nutritious wild plants found in these forests.

Mountains

The mountainous regions of the Pacific Northwest, including the Cascade and Olympic ranges, have diverse microclimates and habitats at various elevations. These areas are known for their striking landscapes and seasonal foraging opportunities.

Alpine Meadows

In the spring and summer, alpine meadows burst into bloom with wildflowers and edible plants. Dandelions *(Taraxacum officinale)*, yampah *(Perideridia spp.),* and wild carrots *(Daucus carota)* are commonly found in these high-altitude areas.

Roots and Tubers

The mountains are home to various edible roots and tubers, like camas *(Camassia spp.),* a traditional food source for indigenous peoples for centuries.

The Pacific Northwest's landscapes are diverse from neighboring regions and house numerous natural resources. It's the combined effect of the following factors that make the Pacific Northwest a one-of-a-kind region:

Climate

The region's maritime climate has mild, wet winters and dry summers, creating ideal conditions for plant growth. The ample rainfall supports lush vegetation, while the feasible temperature allows a long growing season.

Geography

The varied topography, from sea level to high mountains, creates a range of habitats and microclimates. This diversity supports a high level of biodiversity and various edible species.

Soil Fertility

The region's volcanic soil is highly fertile and excellent for plant growth. The areas with past volcanic activity have enriched the soil with minerals, making it a superb place for agriculture and wild plant growth.

Ecological History

Natural disturbances like glaciation, volcanic eruptions, and wildfires have shaped the landscape over millennia. These processes have created a mosaic of habitats supporting a wide array of plant and animal life.

Whether you forage for seaweeds and shellfish along the coast, gather berries and mushrooms in the forests, or explore alpine meadows for edible plants, the Pacific Northwest provides endless opportunities to connect with nature and enjoy the fruits of the land.

Practical Tips for Novices

There's no better way than foraging to connect you with nature and enjoy the bounty of wild foods. However, it requires a careful and knowledgeable approach, particularly when identifying plants. This detailed section provides fundamental concepts of plant identification, practical tips, and essential safety advice to ensure a positive foraging experience.

Basic Concepts of Plant Identification

Accurate plant identification is crucial to forage safely.'

Accurate plant identification is crucial for foraging safely. There's no way around it. Suppose you misidentify a plant and consume a toxic look-alike. In that case, the toxins from the plant can affect your health and, in some cases, even be fatal. Here are the key elements you should be mindful of for proper plant identification:

Habitat Observation

Start by understanding where the plant is growing. Plants have specific habitat preferences. For instance, some proliferate in forests, whereas others need coastal areas. Knowing the typical habitat makes focusing on specific varieties available at the location easier.

Furthermore, remember that plants thrive at different elevations, from sea level to alpine heights. Knowing plant elevation can narrow the identification to a handful of wild edibles.

Detailed Examination of Plant Characteristics

Each plant has various characteristics that make its identification easier.

Leaves

Shape: Plant varieties produce leaves in various shapes, like broad, needle-like, heart-shaped, etc.

Arrangement: Leaves will be arranged alternately, oppositely, or in whorls along the stem.

Edges: Check whether the leaf edges are smooth, serrated, lobed, or toothed.

Venation: The vein's patterns in the leaf can be parallel, pinnate, or palmate.

Texture and Color: Observe if the leaves are hairy, smooth, or waxy, and note their color and variegation.

Stems

Structure: Check if the stem is woody or herbaceous.

Color and Texture: Note distinctive features like color, hairs, or ridges.

Sap: The color and consistency of the sap (e.g., milky, clear, sticky).

Flowers

Structure: Flowers are often key identifiers due to their distinct shape, color, and size.

Number of Petals: Count the petals and note their arrangement.

Inflorescence: Check how flowers are grouped on the plant (e.g., clusters, spikes, umbels).

Fruits and Seeds

Type: Identify the fruit (e.g., berry, nut, capsule).

Color and Size: Note these details, as fruits can vary widely.

Season: Fruit availability can help determine the plant species.

Roots

Type: Roots can be taproots, fibrous, tuberous, etc.

Shape and Size: Plants have distinctive root structures.

Sensory Identification

Smell: Many plants have characteristic smells that can help identification. Gently crush a leaf or stem to release the scent.

Taste: Only taste if you are confident the plant is not toxic. Taste should be the last step, and it should be done with caution.

Using Multiple Sources

Cross-reference with reliable online databases. You can use guides providing detailed descriptions, high-quality photographs, and illustrations. Compare plants with known samples or take pictures and notes to verify later.

Start with Easy-to-Identify Plants

Begin foraging with plants that have distinctive and unmistakable features. Some plants to start with include dandelions, blackberries, and nettles.

Learn from Experienced Foragers

Join local foraging groups and workshops to learn from someone experienced, significantly boosting your knowledge and confidence.

Keep a Foraging Journal

Document your findings with notes and photographs. Include details about the habitat, plant characteristics, and the time of year. This journal can be a reference for future foraging and is a great way to learn without getting bored.

Practice Sustainable Foraging

Only forage the required amount, being mindful of leaving enough for wildlife and regrowth of the wild edibles. Rotating your foraging locations is another sustainable practice preventing overharvesting. Furthermore, avoid harvesting endangered plant species.

Respect Protected Areas

Whether you forage in a public area or on private land, always seek permission before foraging, and know local regulations. Avoid foraging in protected natural reserves and parks where it could be prohibited.

Seasonal Awareness

Plants are available in different seasons. Familiarize yourself with the seasonal patterns of plants in your area. Spring and early summer are great for greens and herbs, while late summer and fall are prime for berries and nuts.

Safety First

Always positively identify a plant before consuming it. Do not eat it if in doubt. Some plants have toxic look-alikes. Furthermore, be aware of potential allergens. Some wild plants can cause skin reactions or other allergic responses.

Avoid foraging in areas with potential pollutants, like roadsides or industrial areas where plants may have absorbed harmful substances.

Ethical Considerations in Foraging

Foraging is not only a means to gather wild foods but also a way to connect deeply with nature.'

Foraging is not only a means to gather wild foods but also a way to connect deeply with nature. As foragers, you have a responsibility to respect the environment and help preserve the delicate balance of ecosystems. Here are ethical considerations to ensure foraging is conducted sustainably and responsibly.

Sustainable Harvesting

Harvest in moderation to ensure plants and fungi can continue to thrive. Never take all the available resources from an area. Many wild plants and fungi are crucial food sources for wildlife. Leave enough behind for animals and other organisms that rely on these resources. Avoid repeatedly harvesting from the same location to prevent overharvesting and allow plant populations to recover.

Minimize Impact

Be mindful of where you step to avoid trampling vegetation and disturbing habitats. Stick to established trails when possible. Use tools that minimize damage to plants and the surrounding environment. For example, using a knife or pruners to cut rather than to pull plants from the ground can cause soil erosion and root damage and kill the plant. Take your waste with you and leave the area as you found it. This includes not disturbing natural features like rocks and logs, which provide a habitat for various organisms.

Know the Status of Species

Learn to identify and avoid rare or endangered plants and fungi. These species need consistent protection to survive. Adhere to local regulations regarding the collection of wild plants and fungi. Contact conservation organizations to learn more about the rules and vulnerable species in the area.

Promote Biodiversity

Focus on harvesting non-invasive, native species that are abundant and vital for the ecosystem. Be aware of invasive species and avoid inadvertently spreading them through your foraging activities.

Educate Yourself

Stay informed about the ecology of the areas you forage in and the plants and fungi you collect. If you travel in a group, educate fellow foragers and the community about sustainable and ethical foraging practices. Promoting awareness keeps the natural resources protected.

Respect Indigenous Knowledge and Lands

Many indigenous cultures have long histories of foraging based on deep ecological knowledge and respect for the land. Learn about and respect these traditions. If you forage on land belonging to indigenous peoples or other communities, seek permission and follow their guidelines and practices.

For example, in the Pacific Northwest, the Coast Salish tribe's rich tradition of foraging shows a deep understanding of and respect for the land. The Coast Salish people have long gathered a variety of wild edibles.

For example, the tribe forages the berries of the Oregon Grape *(Mahonia aquifolium)* and processes them to make medicine.

Follow specific guidelines or protocols provided by the community. This may include limits on how much you can harvest, specific gathering methods, and ensuring you leave enough to sustain those species.

Understand Ecological Roles

Recognize the roles plants and fungi play in their ecosystems. For example, some fungi form symbiotic relationships with trees, and their removal can harm the tree. Consider how removing certain plants or fungi may affect other species, including insects, animals, and microorganisms.

For instance, Matsutake mushrooms are highly prized for their distinct aroma and are found in coniferous forests. These mushrooms form mycorrhizal relationships with various tree species, like pine and Douglas fir. In this symbiotic relationship, the fungus helps the tree absorb water and nutrients from the soil, while the tree provides the fungus with carbohydrates produced through photosynthesis.

Removing matsutake mushrooms can disrupt their symbiotic relationship with trees, potentially affecting their health and growth. Likewise, many insects depend on mushrooms for food and habitat, like beetles and fly larvae that feed on fungal-fruiting bodies. Deer and rodents consume mushrooms as part of their diet.

The right approach here would be to harvest mushrooms selectively and sparingly to ensure the mycelium (the vegetative part of the fungus) remains intact and can continue its symbiotic relationship with trees. Furthermore, soil disturbance should be minimized to preserve the mycorrhizal network and avoid harming other microorganisms.

Support Conservation Efforts

Engage in activities like planting native species or participating in clean-up efforts. Support policies and initiatives aiming to protect natural habitats and biodiversity. You can participate in planting native species like the western red cedar *(Thuja plicata),* Douglas fir *(Pseudotsuga menziesii),* and salal *(Gaultheria shallon)* in areas around Puget Sound. These efforts help restore native habitats, improve biodiversity, and support local wildlife. You can increase the area's biodiversity, improve soil health, and promote conservation practices with the right effort.

Ethically, foraging is the proper way to gather wild foods and develop a respectful and sustainable relationship with nature. Through sustainable harvesting, protecting plant and animal populations, and maintaining ecosystem balance, foraging remains a viable and responsible activity. Respect for the environment and a commitment to preserving ecosystems are the ethos of ethical foraging. As you plan your foraging adventures, carry these principles with you to positively affect your health and witness the beauty of the natural world.

With its lush ecosystems and abundant resources, the Pacific Northwest is an ideal place to begin or continue your foraging expeditions. Every expedition in this region can yield all-natural edibles and profound experiences.

In the chapters to come, you will learn to identify and harvest a wide variety of wild edibles, understand their ecological roles, and discover how to prepare and enjoy them sustainably.

Get ready to unlock the secrets of the Pacific Northwest's natural pantry. Foraging in this region will fill your basket with wild foods and enrich your soul with the beauty and wisdom of nature.

Chapter 2: Tools, Equipment, and Safety

Think back to centuries ago, a day before the first stone tools were invented. Humans hunted small wild animals, probably with their bare hands. Hares were plentiful, but they couldn't always catch one. Insects like ants and beetles were easier to catch but not delicious. Hence, foraging for wild edibles may have come to their rescue.

Early humans foraged for anything healthy they could lay their hands on, from nuts and acorns to nettles and seeds. Even without tools, they were strong enough to collect edibles. Did you know their strength and agility exceeded modern-day athletes? Nevertheless, they may have faced many problems because foraging without tools isn't easy.

Let's Get Ready

Like early humans, you can forage with your bare hands wearing any clothing. However, wild plants can be very stubborn. They have tough stems that may not come off, no matter how hard you pull. You can try to twist them free, but you could damage the plant instead. You can easily cut them with a sharp tool like scissors.

Foraging with your bare hands takes a lot of time since you are mostly twisting or pulling to collect the edibles. You may need at least 10 seconds to break each small edible free. Also, there is a significant risk you will pull the entire plant, including its roots. Did you know that unnecessarily uprooting plants can make the land infertile?

On the other hand, the work becomes faster with tools because snipping or cutting doesn't take more than a second, and you don't risk uprooting the plant. They greatly reduce environmental damage by ensuring a cleaner harvest. Therefore, the right equipment makes you an efficient and caring forager.

Sometimes, you need roots, especially those of medicinal plants. Suppose you dig the soil with your hands. In that case, you may accidentally unearth a larger area, damaging the rest of the vegetation nearby. Tools can help you dig up roots without damaging the surrounding plants.

A critical aspect of foraging for beginners is safety. In the Pacific Northwest, there are many thorny and dangerous plants. Pulling them out with your bare hands can result in scrapes and cuts. Tools and safety gear, like shears and gloves, are recommended for foraging.

Furthermore, carrying your collected edibles home can be risky. Berries and fruits are soft and mushy, and many plants and mushrooms are easily damaged in a confined space. You may end up with a rotten mixture if you keep your edibles in your pocket. Storing them in the right container during transportation will ensure your foraging efforts don't go to waste.

Responsible Foraging

Any foraging tool is like a double-edged sword. It can easily harm the environment and bring efficiency to your foraging practice. You can't use your knife or scythe to cut plants willy-nilly. Carving a path through an especially dense forest differs from clearing an area to find valuable plants. You may want that elusive little plant, but it doesn't give you the right to destroy other plants.

Use your tools and equipment so that they do minimum damage to the environment. Respect nature; it will give you plenty of foraging edibles in return. For example, a stick or a spade can be used to sift through the surrounding vegetation to find the desired plant instead of cutting it all down.

Essential Foraging Tools

Given the profound importance of foraging tools and equipment, you may think you must carry a couple of heavy bags. This isn't true. Experienced foragers travel light. You should prepare not only for foraging and safety but also to walk long distances. You can never be sure where your desired edibles are in the wild of the Pacific Northwest.

All your essential foraging tools should fit into a small backpack. You will feel even lighter carrying it all in a multipurpose, pocketed belt.

- **Knife:** Foraging without a knife is like diving without scuba gear. You may manage for a while, but you will have to head back home soon. Foraging without a knife is three times as difficult. You can easily cut plants and mushrooms, carve a path through growing weeds, and protect yourself against possible predators with a knife.

Pick a knife especially made for foraging. A fungi knife is a small, multipurpose tool, usually with a serrated edge on one side for cleaning mossy beds or collected edibles and a brush at the bottom for clearing the soil. If you pull out a mushroom, another won't grow in its place. You can make a clean cut with a fungi knife, leaving the mycelium (root-like structure) and taking only the edible part of the fungi. Also, a Swiss Army knife has many uses in the wild.

- **Shears or Scissors:** What can't be cut with a single knife can be cut with two. Foraging or pruning shears are useful for cutting stubborn plants or thick stems and are small enough to fit in your pocket. You could use kitchen scissors, but they won't be strong enough to cut the hardy plants.

What can't be cut with a single knife can be cut with two.[7]

- **Basket or Bag:** If you are foraging in your backyard or at a nearby park, you won't need a bag for that handful of edibles. However, if you are heading to the forests or mountains, usually far from civilization in the Pacific Northwest, you will likely collect at least a week's supply of edibles. Don't put them in your backpack to prevent damage.

Use a mesh or specialized foraging bag with multiple compartments to properly arrange your collectibles.'

Edibles need a breathable material to keep them from rotting. Use a mesh bag or a specialized foraging bag with multiple compartments to properly arrange your collectibles.

- **Field Guides:** The edible plant population in the region is vast. Unless you have a photographic memory, you can't hope to remember everything you learned in this book. What if you forget what the arrowhead plant looks like? Even worse, what if you mistake an edible camas plant for a death camas plant, which is highly poisonous?

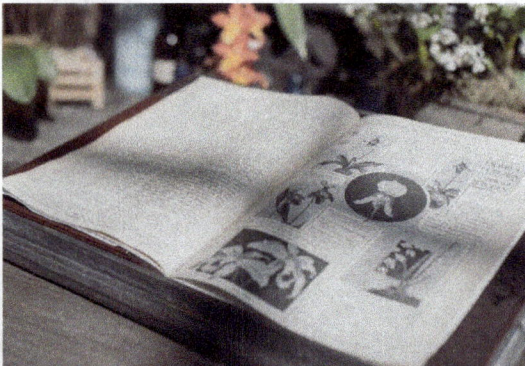

Take this field guide along to identify plants and avoid poisonous look-alikes properly.'

Take field guides along to identify plants and avoid poisonous look-alikes properly. You can refer to it for quick tips you missed during your first read or scan the index for the plant you wish to know more about. Additionally, *keep a local field guide specific to your region.* It will go into greater detail about the edibles found in and around your city or town. Store an eBook copy on your smartphone for easier reference.

Popular Field Guides:

- *The Forager's Kitchen* – Fiona Bird
- *Wild Food* – Roger Phillips
- *Food for Free* - Richard Mabey
- *Forage Field Guide* – Purdue University
- *The Forager's Harvest* – Samuel Thayer

- **First Aid Kit:** The wilderness of the Pacific Northwest often experiences a harsh climate, from incredibly high temperatures of around 90°F in the afternoon to a freezingly cold environment post-dusk. The wild poses a risk of getting hurt, slipping on wet surfaces, getting pricked by thorny plants, and catching ailments due to extreme temperatures like hypothermia and dehydration.

Every basic first aid kit contains antiseptics, bandages, ointments, pain relievers, cold packs, etc.[10]

Every basic first aid kit contains antiseptics, bandages, ointments, pain relievers, cold packs, etc. Additional items to consider are tweezers to remove thorns, antihistamines to relieve insect bites, burn gel if foraging in the afternoon during summer, and personal medications or specific animal bite medications for your area.

- **Eating and Drinking:** Depending on the area, you may not need to carry snacks or water; you could eat some of your collected edibles and drink water from nearby streams. Fruit and berries are also a great source of hydration.

Your snacks in emergencies.[ii]

However, there may be barely any plants left for foraging, especially during spring and fall when your fellow foragers come in large numbers. You may get stuck in one place during heavy rains or excessive snowfall.

In such situations, snacks and water bottles are lifesavers in emergencies. However, take care not to litter. Store the waste in your backpack.

Prioritizing Safety

The landscape of the Pacific Northwest is beautiful in all seasons but incredibly stunning in spring and fall. The coastal areas feature cliffs and dense rainforests. These forests often extend inland with remarkable changes in the tree types, where you will find plenty of ferns, shrubs, and mushrooms for foraging.

The mountain ranges, particularly the Cascades, are ripe with numerous plants and fruits, even lush alpine meadows. The terrain dramatically changes east, scaling vast deserts rich with wildflowers. Valleys, rivers, lakes, and many other areas are a forager's delight.

However, this beauty is filled with many dangers for the negligent forager. While admiring the bountiful terrain, don't forget to be always alert. Learn about the local plants, animals, insects, and other creatures. Familiarize yourself with the specific locations you plan to forage. Seek advice from experienced foragers or people who have visited the place beforehand.

To avoid accidental consumption of toxic plants, be 100% certain of their edibility and safety. Many edible species have toxic look-alikes. Keep referring to chapter 4 of this book while foraging. Also, the weather in the Pacific Northwest can change without warning. Be prepared for heavy rainfall in spring and snowfall in the fall. Always check the weather forecast before heading out.

Watch for wildlife, unstable terrain, and other potential hazards (discussed in the next section) while foraging. Wear the right clothing for the corresponding weather. Don't forage in your home attire.

If you're pricked or cut, care for it using your first aid kit. Don't let the wound fester, or it might get infected. Are you feeling heady or nauseous? Rest for a while under a tree or a shady area and keep hydrated. If the feeling persists, leave and go straight to a nearby doctor. You may have been unknowingly poisoned.

Once you have collected all the foraged items in a breathable container, don't eat them immediately. Go to a nearby stream and wash them thoroughly. After reaching home, wash and store them in appropriate containers (discussed later). For instance, berries and mushrooms should be stored in the fridge.

Potential Hazards

A major hazard of foraging in the wild is eating poisonous plants. Did you know there are over 700 species of poisonous plants in the U.S. alone? An estimated 17,000 plant species are in the country. The chances are that every 25th plant species you forage will be poisonous, but only if you know nothing about plants.

Certain venomous plants may resemble edibles, like false morels (fungi).[18]

Go through the extensive list of edibles in this book specific to the Pacific Northwest, noting each plant's unique characteristics to ensure you don't pluck unknowns while foraging. Also, certain venomous plants may resemble edibles, like false morels (fungi) and water hemlock. As a beginner, avoid gathering plant species with toxic look-alikes.

However, inanimate plant life isn't the only danger in the region. Ferocious bears prowl the land, with their thick fur protecting them from the extreme cold. Their strength and unpredictability make them among the most dangerous animals in the Pacific Northwest. Black bears are more common but are usually harmless. Grizzly bears are found in northern Washington and the mountainous regions but are scarce.

Bears are carnivores but don't typically eat humans. They will attack you only if provoked, so don't alarm them if you cross paths with one. Back away slowly with your arms on your head without making sudden movements.

Carry a bear spray and keep it ready, but don't fire just yet. If the bear follows you and gets within 30 feet, aim it at their face and fire. It will burn their eyes and cause them to suffocate slightly, but it won't cause permanent harm. You can run away while they struggle with the spray's effects.

Another dangerous animal is the cougar, usually found in rainforests. They prefer solitude, so their sightings are rare. However, they might attack you if you stumble into their territory. They feed on easily attainable prey like deer and small mammals but won't hesitate to pounce if threatened.

Avoid foraging in rainforests at dusk or dawn when cougars are most active. Don't run or turn your back on them. Maintain eye contact and stand straight with your arms stretched upward. If they attack, fight back with whatever tools you have.

Little creatures like bees and spiders are a cause for concern. Their bites can develop rashes and lead to allergic reactions. Avoid foraging near hives or webs.

The non-living world can be equally hazardous if you're not careful. The region's diverse landscapes include steep slopes, dense forests, and rugged coastlines. Be cautious of slippery rocks, loose soil, and uneven ground. Also, the weather is prone to change rapidly. One moment, it may be as clear as day, but the next, there might be heavy rainfall or thick fog.

Appropriate Clothing

The weather is often unpredictable in the Pacific Northwest, especially in spring. You will have headed out in the bright morning sunshine but could return drenched in the heavy rains an hour later. Moreover, the weather is usually cold in the early morning and post-afternoon.

Wear multiple layers, with woolen fabric at the base to absorb sweat and an insulating fleece jacket over it. Wear a waterproof jacket if it's snowing or raining. In a mild climate, wear a long-sleeve shirt made from lightweight and breathable fabric to protect your arms from scratches, insect bites, and sun exposure.

Choose durable, lightweight, quick-drying nylon pants for the lower body. Waterproof hiking boots are ideal for any terrain, from the mountain ranges to the deserts. Pair these with moisture-wicking socks. It's advisable to bring an extra pair of socks in case your first pair gets wet. Top it off with hiking gaiters to protect your lower legs and ankles from insects, snakes, and the cold.

Wear a hat for sun protection if you plan to forage only in the afternoon. Carry a warm beanie if your trip might extend into late evening. Gloves protect your hands from thorns, insects, and the cold. A scarf can keep your neck safe in any weather, whether the scorching sun or the chilly snow. As a precaution, carry a packable rain poncho for sudden rain showers and thermal undergarments for extra warmth in colder conditions.

Additional Equipment

The essential tools listed are necessary for a successful foraging endeavor. However, the following additional equipment will enhance your experience and solidify your safety:

- **Magnifying Glasses:** A standard magnifying glass of up to 10x magnification will help you see the small characteristics of plants to identify them better. It could mean the difference between life and death, avoiding venomous look-alikes whose differentiating characteristics are often minute. If you're interested in studying the plant and insect life in the region, go for a higher magnification of around 30x.

A standard magnifying glass of up to 10x magnification will help you see the small characteristics of plants to identify them better.[18]

- **Containers for Safe Transport:** Your basic foraging wicker basket is ideal for holding your edibles, but while going back home (walking, biking, driving, etc.), they may get damaged, mixed, or crushed under the weight of other edibles. You need a compartmentalized container with a cover for safe storage during transport.

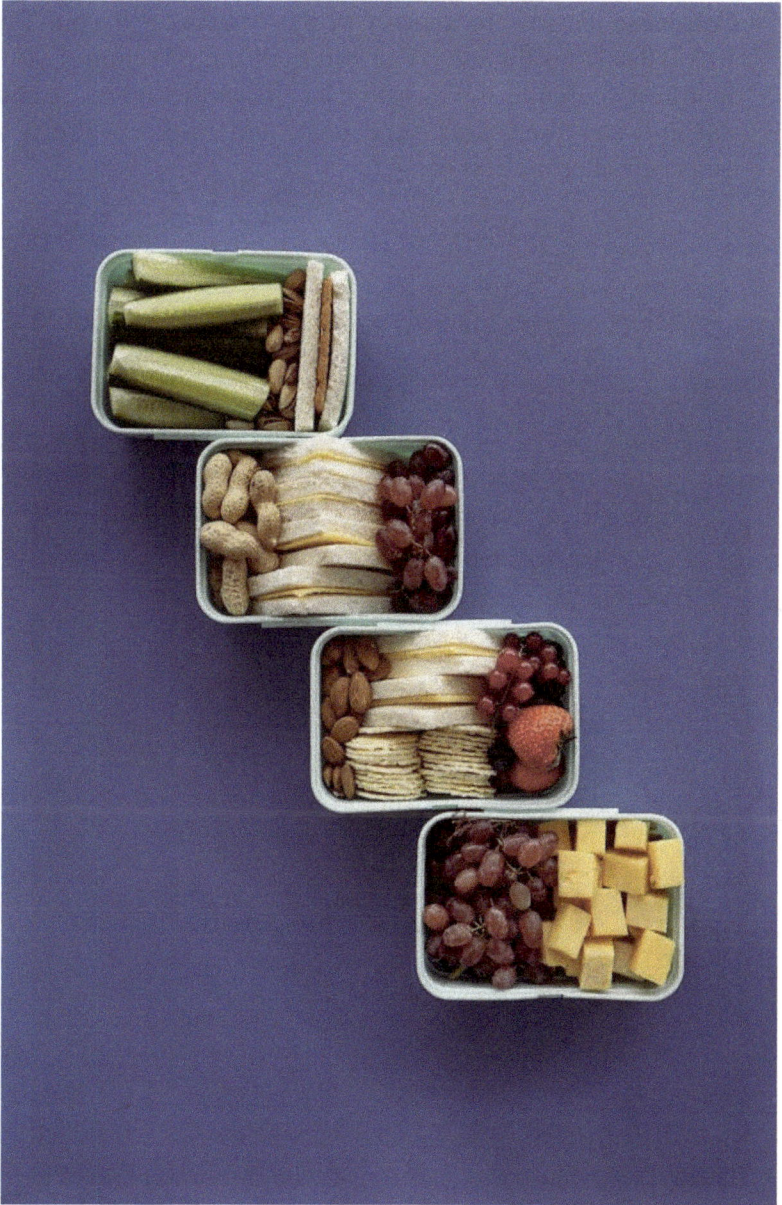

Consider buying a food-grade plastic container for carrying delicate items like berries and fruits.¹⁴

Consider buying a food-grade plastic container with compartments for carrying delicate items like berries and fruits. The compartments are great for organizing the edibles and preventing them from getting damaged. You can use a mesh bag for mushrooms.

- **Compass:** It's easy to get lost in the wilderness if your foraging area is far from the city. You can't tell the direction if you have ventured deep into the forest or far out in the desert. A compass will indicate where you came from and where you're heading, especially after the sun has set.

A compass will indicate where you came from and where you're heading, especially after the sun has set.[15]

The Pacific Northwest has a significant magnetic declination, the angle difference between true and magnetic north. Find the local declination for your area and adjust your compass before heading out. Note the direction from which you entered the foraging area and check your compass from time to time.

- **Map:** Smartphones have pre-installed digital maps, but your foraging area may not have internet range. Download a map of the area beforehand. The GPS navigator will indicate where you are even without the internet. Alternatively, you can buy a paper map of the region at a local bookstore. Mark the point of your entry into the area and keep tracking your path manually at regular intervals.

Download a map of the area beforehand.[16]

- **Leather Gloves:** These gloves can help you dig for roots, and tools like shovels, picks, spades, etc., can ease the process. Ensure they are compact enough to fit in your pocket or backpack.

Gloves can help you dig for roots, and tools like shovels, picks, spades, etc., can ease the process.[17]

Tips on Maintaining and Caring for Tools

Tools that haven't been maintained can become useless in a matter of weeks. You don't have to do much. Merely clean them after every use. Use a dry cloth to remove dirt and debris and wash them in a disinfectant, like bleach. Dry them with a clean cloth to avoid corrosion.

Sharpen your knives and shears every few months or whenever you feel the blade is blunt. Apply a light coat of oil to metal parts to prevent rust before storage. Don't keep them open in the garage. Stash them in a toolbox to avoid environmental damage. A sheath or other protective covering is even better.

You can put your mesh bags, cloth bags, and foraging clothes in the washer, but don't add your regular clothes, or they may become stained. Clean your foraging baskets with soap and water and hang them to air dry.

Remember: While you can forage without tools, using them will enhance your experience and keep you safe from natural hazards. The right tools and equipment will protect the environment as you learn to forage sustainably without damaging surrounding plants or uprooting them completely.

Chapter 3: Seasonal Foraging in the Pacific Northwest

In the Pacific Northwest, the foraging landscape is dynamic and ever-changing, with each season bringing in various wild edibles and experiences. As you already know, the region is extremely biodiverse, and its climate supports the growth of wild plants almost throughout the year.

The Cyclical Nature of Nature's Bounty

The Pacific Northwest's seasonal shifts are pronounced, with each part of the year bringing forth plants and fungi ripe for harvesting.[18]

The Pacific Northwest's seasonal shifts are pronounced, with each part of the year bringing forth plants and fungi ripe for harvesting. Understanding these seasonal patterns is essential for foragers looking to make the most of what nature offers.

Spring Season

As winter retreats, spring breathes new life into the Pacific Northwest. The forests and meadows awaken, producing various edibles to forage.

There will be an abundance of young, tender greens like dandelion leaves, miner's lettuce, and nettles. These plants are among the first to appear, providing essential nutrients after the long winter. Violets and elderflowers bloom, adding vibrant colors and delicate flavors to foragers' baskets.

Spring marks the arrival of sought-after mushrooms like morels, which thrive in the warming soil and are highly prized for their unique taste.

Summer

Summer is a time for abundance in the Pacific Northwest, with many wild edibles reaching their peak. The region's forests and meadows are bursting with various berries, including blackberries, huckleberries, and salmonberries. These sweet and tart fruits are the highlight of summer foraging.

Many edible weeds, like purslane and lamb's quarters, are at their best during summer, providing nutritious and plentiful options. Summer is the season for herbs and edible flowers, like wild mint and nasturtiums, which enhance the flavor of many dishes.

Fall

As the days grow shorter and cooler, the Pacific Northwest still provides a rich harvest of wild edibles. It's the best time for gathering hazelnuts, acorns, and various nuts, which can be processed and stored for the winter months. The fall rains bring forth another flush of mushrooms, including chanterelles and porcini, favorites among foragers. Wild apples, pears, and root vegetables like camas bulbs reach their prime in fall, offering hearty and sustaining foods for the coming winter.

Winter

Winter may seem like a quiet time for foraging in many regions, but the Pacific Northwest still holds subtle opportunities. Certain parts of evergreen trees, like young tips and pine nuts, can be foraged during winter. In some areas, you can find oyster mushrooms during mild winters.

The ever-changing landscape of the Pacific Northwest means that no two foraging experiences are the same. The transition of the seasons, weather patterns, and local ecosystems creates a constantly shifting list of wild edibles. You must be adaptable and observant and learn to read nature's subtle signs indicating what is available and when.

Spring in the Pacific Northwest

Spring in the Pacific Northwest is a time of renewal and rejuvenation as nature shakes off the remnants of winter and pops out with vibrant new life. The transition from the cold months to the warmth of spring is a spectacle to watch. The colors, scents, and sounds are enchanting and enough to awaken the senses.

Once cloaked in the coldness of winter, forests stir with signs of life. Dormant trees bud with the branches producing delicate blossoms, marking the arrival of spring. Once covered in a blanket of fallen leaves, the forest floor comes alive with a carpet of greenery as tender shoots push their way through the moist earth, reaching eagerly toward the sun. In the meadows and mountain slopes, colorful wildflowers unfurl their petals in a dazzling display.

Bounty of Spring Forage

While spring is in its early stages, there are signs of abundance for those who know where to look. Patches of tender young greens emerge in the forest, their vibrant hues contrasting against moss-covered logs and clearings. For example, with their serrated leaves and stinging hairs, Nettles are among the first to appear on the forest bed.

Likewise, in the damp and shaded recesses of the forest, there is a high chance of locating the elusive morel mushroom with its distinctive honeycomb cap standing out against the forest floor. These mushrooms, known for their rich, nutty flavor and meaty texture, are highly prized by culinary enthusiasts and foragers, who eagerly anticipate their brief but bountiful season.

As spring progresses, the landscape evolves, producing new wild edibles daily. Along the banks of creeks and streams, clusters of wild onions and ramps emerge, their pungent aroma filling the air. The first signs of early berries appear in the meadows and open spaces, with salmonberries and wild strawberries dangling from their stems, their sweet juices ripening in the warm spring sun.

Exercise Caution in Spring Foraging

While the allure of spring foraging is undeniable, you must approach this season with caution and respect. Many plants and fungi are in the early growth stages, and some may not yet be safe for consumption. Foragers must exercise caution when identifying and harvesting wild edibles, avoiding toxic look-alikes, and ensuring they leave behind enough of each species to allow for natural regeneration.

Over-harvesting during this fragile time can disrupt the delicate balance of ecosystems, leading to long-term harm to plant and animal populations. Be mindful of the environmental impact and stick to sustainable harvesting practices that minimize your footprint on the land.

Always forage with patience, caution, and respect, regardless of season. While you can forage various wild edibles in spring, it may be wise to wait a few months for the full bounty of summer and fall to unfold.

The Summer Landscape

The landscape transforms remarkably as spring gracefully shifts to summer in the Pacific Northwest. Warmer temperatures and longer days push the forests to their greenery peak, and mountain meadows burst into life with an array of vibrant wildflowers. This season brings various edibles waiting to be discovered for foragers.

With the arrival of summer, the Pacific Northwest becomes a stunning paradise, teeming with life and vitality. Once filled with blossoms and blooming flowers, the forests become cloaked in emerald green trees, their canopies providing shade from the sun's warm effect. Shafts of light filter through the dense foliage, illuminating the forest floor with patches of golden sunlight and casting a magical glow over the landscape.

In the mountain meadows and alpine slopes, a riot of color erupts as wildflowers burst into bloom. Lupines, paintbrushes, and columbines sway gently in the breeze, their vibrant hues creating a stunning contrast against the backdrop of rugged peaks and clear blue skies. Bees and butterflies fly from flower to flower, pollinating the blooms and ensuring the continuation of life.

Abundant Berries and Mushrooms

Summer in the Pacific Northwest is synonymous with abundant wild berries, with favorites like huckleberries, blackberries, and raspberries ripening to perfection. These juicy and flavorful fruits are a highlight of the season, attracting foragers from far and wide who eagerly fill their baskets with nature's sweet treasures. Along the forested trails and mountain slopes, patches of ripe berries thrive. The berries look like precious jewels waiting to be discovered in the sunlight.

Meanwhile, edible mushrooms continue to flourish in the damp and shaded recesses of the forest. Varieties like chanterelles, porcini, and oyster mushrooms thrive in warm, humid summer conditions, their delicate caps peeking out from beneath layers of leaf litter and moss. If you have a keen eye and a bit of luck, you can find these culinary delights hidden in the forest floor's debris.

Impact of Weather and Landscape on Foraging Practices

The weather and landscape are significant in shaping foraging and harvesting practices during the summer months. Warmer temperatures and longer days provide ideal conditions for plant growth, resulting in a bountiful harvest of wild edibles. You must take advantage of this abundance while being mindful of your action's environmental impact.

Explore the dense undergrowth, wild plants, and trees for ripe berries, edible plants, and prized mushrooms in the forests. However, you must exercise caution when harvesting to avoid damaging the delicate plants and fungi that call the forest home. Furthermore, you must be aware of potential hazards like steep terrain, wildlife encounters, and changing weather conditions, ensuring your safety while exploring the wilderness.

Harvest Time in the Pacific Northwest

As summer gracefully gives way to fall in the Pacific Northwest, the landscape changes drastically again. The vibrant greens of summer are replaced by the fiery hues of autumn foliage, painting the forests and mountain slopes with reds, oranges, and yellows. You can forage most mushroom varieties in this season.

Fall in the Pacific Northwest is a feast for the senses, as the air fills with the scent of fallen leaves and the earthy aroma of damp forest floors. The trees with green foliage wither, the leaves turn red, orange and gold and the humidity increases.While summer's berry bounty may be waning, fall offers a variety of late-season berries and nuts for foragers to enjoy. Elderberries, with their tart flavor and deep purple hue, are prized for their culinary versatility and medicinal properties, while late-season blackberries offer a final burst of sweetness before the onset of winter. Hazelnuts and chestnuts ripen on the trees, their rich flavors and satisfying crunch adding a touch of autumnal warmth.

Best Edibles to Forage During Fall

Foragers in the Pacific Northwest are spoiled for choice during autumn harvests, with a plethora of wild edibles waiting to be discovered. Some of the best edibles to forage during this season include:

Mushrooms: Chanterelles, porcini, and lobster mushrooms are among the most sought-after varieties for their rich flavors and culinary versatility.

Late-Season Berries: Elderberries and late-season blackberries give you a kick of sweetness, perfect for jams, jellies, and desserts.

Nuts: Hazelnuts and chestnuts are ready for harvest. Their rich flavors and satisfying crunch make them a nutritious and delicious addition to your foraging basket.

Winter Foraging in the Pacific Northwest

As winter settles over the Pacific Northwest, the landscape transforms, with cooler temperatures and precipitation bringing a quiet stillness to the region. While wild edibles may be less abundant during this season, a handful of wild edibles are waiting to be discovered.

The Pacific Northwest has many deciduous trees and evergreen forests. However, snowfall in winter blankets the higher elevations, transforming the area into a winter wonderland covered in white. At lower elevations, rain and fog shroud the landscape in a veil of mist, creating an atmosphere where life thrives without a hitch.

Winter greens like miner's lettuce can be found in milder coastal areas. Also, oyster mushrooms cling to the damp bark of fallen trees or hiding beneath layers of moss and debris.

Awareness of Winter Hazards

Knowing potential hazards and challenges is essential for beginner foragers venturing into the winter. The weather in the Pacific Northwest can be unpredictable during the winter months, with sudden changes in temperature and precipitation. You must dress warmly and be prepared for inclement weather, including rain, snow, and cold temperatures.

Furthermore, hazards like slippery trails, unstable terrain, and avalanches can occur at higher elevations. The best approach in adverse climate conditions is to stick to the designated paths and use adequate gear for better navigation. Also, being mindful of wildlife encounters is essential, as many animals are more actively searching for food during winter.

Harvesting Considerations

When harvesting wild edibles during winter, you must be mindful of your action's impact on the environment. Winter greens and mushrooms may be less abundant, so practice sustainable harvesting techniques for the continued health of natural ecosystems.

Foraging Safety Tips in the Pacific Northwest

Whether venturing into forests in spring, bountiful meadows in summer, vibrant foliage in fall, or quiet winter landscapes, you must prioritize safety to ensure a successful and enjoyable experience. Here are essential tips to stay safe while foraging in each season:

Spring

Spring weather can be unpredictable, with chilly mornings giving way to warm afternoons.[19]

- Spring weather can be unpredictable, with chilly mornings giving way to warm afternoons. Dressing in layers allows you to adjust to changing temperatures throughout the day. Go for three-layered clothing: a wool base layer to keep sweat at bay, a fleece mid-layer shirt for insulation, and a breathable and waterproof jacket to protect against rain and wind. Refer to the previous chapter if you are unsure what gear to pack for foraging.

- Forest floors can be muddy and uneven in spring, so wear waterproof and sturdy footwear with good traction to prevent slips and falls. Use hiking poles or a wooden stick to aid in navigating uneven terrain.

- In spring, ticks become more active in wooded areas, posing a potential health risk to foragers. Take precautions to prevent tick bites by wearing long sleeves, pants tucked into socks, and insect repellent containing DEET or picaridin. Perform regular tick checks on yourself and your companions during and after foraging trips, paying close attention to hidden areas like the scalp, armpits, and groin. If you find a tick attached to your skin, use fine-tipped tweezers to carefully remove it, grasping it as close to the skin surface as possible and pulling upward with steady pressure. Take an antihistamine and a painkiller from your emergency first aid box if you feel redness, swelling, and a slight burning sensation.

- Proper hydration is vital during outdoor activities, even in cooler spring temperatures. Carry an adequate water or hydration system, and drink regularly throughout your foraging excursion. Aim to consume at least eight ounces of water every 20-30 minutes to prevent dehydration and maintain peak performance. Monitor your fluid intake and urine output as indicators of hydration status, adjusting your drinking habits accordingly to stay hydrated and energized.

- While spring heralds the emergence of various mushroom species in the Pacific Northwest, exercising caution when foraging for fungi is essential. Many edible mushrooms have toxic counterparts closely resembling them, making accurate identification crucial. Unless you possess extensive knowledge and experience in mushroom foraging, refrain from harvesting wild mushrooms for consumption. Consider joining guided mushroom forays or consulting with mycological experts to safely explore the world of fungi.

- Study local flora before heading out to forage. Invest in field guides specific to the region or attend workshops led by experienced foragers to improve plant identification skills. Focus on learning key features of edible and medicinal plants, common look-alikes, and toxic species. Pay attention to nuances in leaf shape, flower color, stem texture, and growth habits to accurately identify plants in the wild.

- Poisonous plants pose a significant risk to foragers, especially beginners. Learn to recognize common toxic plants, like poison hemlock, foxglove, and deadly nightshade. Familiarize yourself with these plants' distinguishing features and growth habitats to avoid accidental ingestion. If uncertain about a plant's identity, err on the side of caution and refrain from harvesting or consuming it.

Summer

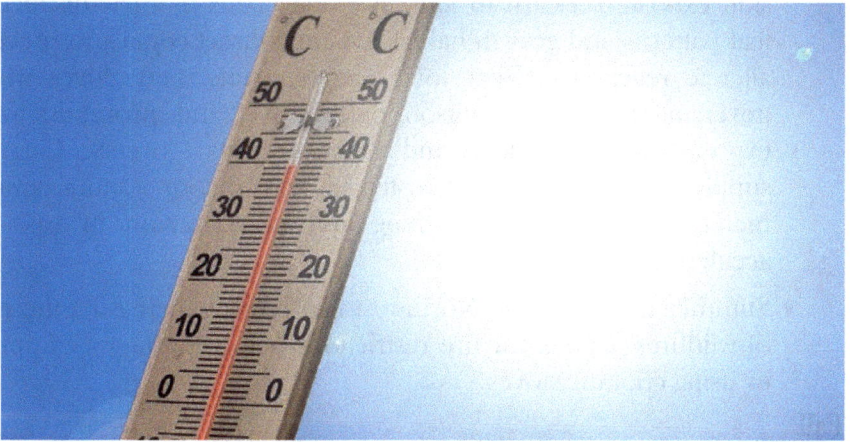

Summer brings increased sun exposure and higher temperatures to the Pacific Northwest, necessitating effective sun protection measures.[20]

- Summer brings increased sun exposure and higher temperatures to the Pacific Northwest, necessitating effective sun protection measures. Wear lightweight, breathable clothing that covers exposed skin to minimize sunburn risk. Wear a wide-brimmed hat to shade your face and neck and UV-blocking sunglasses to protect your eyes from harmful UV rays. Apply a broad-spectrum sunscreen with SPF 30 or higher to exposed skin, reapplying every two hours or after swimming or sweating profusely.

- Regardless of the season, staying hydrated is crucial. Carry plenty of water and consider bringing electrolyte-rich snacks or drinks to replenish lost fluids.

- The diverse ecosystems of the Pacific Northwest are home to a wide range of wildlife species, including bears, cougars, and venomous snakes. When foraging in natural habitats, maintain awareness of your surroundings and watch for signs of animal activity, such as tracks, scat, and territorial markings. Make noise while hiking by talking, singing, or clapping hands to alert wildlife to your presence and minimize the risk of startling or surprising animals. Store food securely in airtight containers and avoid leaving food scraps or scented items unattended to prevent attracting wildlife to your campsite or foraging area.

- Poison oak and ivy are common toxic plants in the Pacific Northwest wooded areas, posing a risk of contact dermatitis upon skin exposure. Learn to identify these plants by their distinctive leaf patterns and growth habits, avoiding direct contact to prevent allergic reactions. Wear long sleeves, pants, and gloves when traversing areas with poison oak or ivy, and promptly wash exposed skin with soap and water if contact occurs. Carry a supply of topical corticosteroid cream or antihistamine medication to alleviate itching and inflammation in case of accidental exposure.

- Summer in the Pacific Northwest can be dry, increasing the risk of wildfires. Check for fire restrictions before starting a campfire or using cooking stoves.

Fall

Fall weather can be unpredictable, with chilly mornings and evenings.[31]

- Fall weather can be unpredictable, with chilly mornings and evenings. Dress in layers and bring a waterproof jacket to stay warm and dry.

- Autumn foliage and rain showers can create slippery conditions on hiking trails and forest paths, increasing the risk of slips, trips, and falls. Exercise caution when navigating wet or leaf-covered surfaces, using sturdy footwear with grippy outsoles to maintain traction on slippery terrain. Consider using trekking poles or walking sticks for added stability and balance, especially when traversing steep inclines or uneven terrain. Avoid rushing and maintain a deliberate pace to minimize the risk of accidents and injuries while foraging in the fall.

- Daylight hours shorten as fall progresses. Plan your foraging trips accordingly, and bring a headlamp or flashlight if you're out after dark.

- The risk of minor injuries increases with changing weather and terrain. Carry a basic first aid kit with essentials, like bandages, antiseptic wipes, and pain relievers.

Winter

Winter temperatures in the Pacific Northwest are cold, especially at higher elevations.[22]

- Winter temperatures in the Pacific Northwest are cold, especially at higher elevations. Wear insulated, moisture-wicking clothing and bring extra layers, hats, gloves, and waterproof boots to stay warm and dry.

- Higher elevations may be covered in snow and ice during winter. Use traction devices like micro-spikes or crampons on icy trails and a trekking pole for added stability.

- If you venture into avalanche terrain, check avalanche forecasts and carry essential safety gear, including a beacon, shovel, and probe. Consider taking an avalanche safety course if you plan to explore avalanche-prone areas.

- Always let someone know your intended route and expected return time, especially when venturing into remote or unfamiliar areas. Carry a fully charged cell phone and consider bringing a personal locator beacon for safety.

Foraging in the Pacific Northwest offers many experiences throughout the seasons, from spring's vibrant renewal to winter's quiet introspection. By prioritizing safety and preparedness, foragers can fully immerse themselves in the region's beauty and bounty, minimizing risks and ensuring a memorable and rewarding experience.

Chapter 4: Wild Edible Plants of the Pacific Northwest

The seasonal variations of the Pacific Northwest are unpredictable, but the landscape is always pristine. Every season is the perfect time to forage if you have an eye for beauty. Now, it's time to develop an eye for plants and other edibles. This chapter will take you through edible plants, fruits, trees, etc., available in the region as you learn how to identify them and explore their nutritional benefits.

Greens and Shoots

Dandelion Greens *(Taraxacum officinale)*

Dandelions are among the most popular herbal medicines in the world.[a]

Dandelions (genus *Taraxacum*) are among the most instantly recognizable plants on Earth – but although almost everyone knows what they look like, far fewer people know that they're also extremely useful plants: all parts of the plant (besides the seeds) are edible and nutritious.

Dandelion leaves are deeply lobed, with backward-pointing "teeth" that look like a grappling hook from afar. Like most plants in the sunflower family (Asteraceae), what appear to be the "flowers" are actually compound inflorescences, each comprising dozens of individual florets. The capitula are borne on unbranched, hollow stalks, which bleed bitter white sap when broken. Only true dandelions have hollow stalks, which can help distinguish them from common lookalikes.

Dandelions tolerate an enormous range of growing conditions, but they thrive in sunny, disturbed soils, from roadsides and pastures to meadows and waterways – anywhere there is sufficient sunlight and moisture. They are among the first flowers to appear in spring, but can appear at almost any time of year, especially after a spell of mild, wet weather.

- **Nutritional Benefits:** Dandelion greens (leaves) are rich in vitamins A, C, and K, calcium, iron, and potassium. They can be eaten raw in salads or cooked. The flowers can be simmered in water and made into jelly or wine, while the roots have been used medicinally and as a coffee substitute.

- **Potential Look-Alikes:** A number of closely related plants may be mistaken for dandelion – most notably cat's ear (*Hypochaeris radicata*), which is invasive in the Pacific Northwest. Though also edible, the leaves of cat's ear are conspicuously hairy, and have wavy rather than toothed margins. When in doubt, look for a plant in bloom and check for the dandelion's characteristic hollow stem.

- **Poisonous Counterparts:** Although they have no toxic lookalikes, foragers should still exercise care when harvesting dandelions, as they can absorb toxins from their environment, from engine exhaust to chemical pesticides and even heavy metals. For this reason, always harvest from undeveloped areas, and avoid places that are likely to be exposed to these pollutants.

Cat's ear (Hypochaeris radicata), an introduced plant often confused with dandelion. Unlike true dandelions, cat's ear has branching flower stalks and wavy leaf margins. [24]

Miner's Lettuce *(Claytonia perfoliata)*

Miner's lettuce is one of the earliest edible plants to emerge in the spring, and is easily identified by its unusual succuluent leaves. [25]

Miner's lettuce can be easily identified by its succulent leaves, which take two forms: the long, spatula-shaped basal leaves emerge first, later followed by *cauline* or stem leaves, which are fused around the stems like little cups. The tiny white (rarely pinkish) flowers bloom from the center of the upper leaf, appearing to pierce through it. It has long, slender, reddish stems.

Miner's lettuce grows best in moist, shaded environments, especially west of the Cascades. It emerges very early in spring, often while snow is still on the ground, and finishes blooming before spring is over. Avoid harvesting plants with flowers, as they tend to be bitter.

- **Nutritional Benefits:** Miner's lettuce is rich in vitamins C and A and iron and is a good source of omega-3 fatty acids. You can eat its leaves and stems raw in salads and sandwiches.

- **Potential Look-Alikes:** The closely related pink purslane (*C. sibirica*) can appear similar to miner's lettuce, but it has bright pink flowers larger, broader leaves. It's also edible, and can harvested throughout the summer, long after miner's lettuce is gone.

- **Poisonous Counterparts:** None.

Goosefoot *(Chenopodium album)*

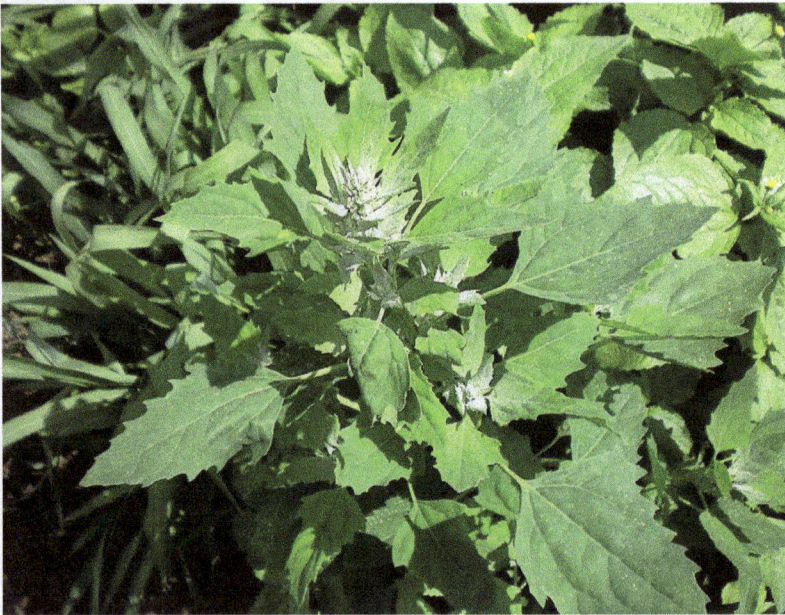

Lamb's quarters have diamond-shaped or triangular leaves with teeth-like edges.[26]

Goosefoot is a large, bushy annual with serrated, diamond-shaped or triangular leaves that look a little like a goose's foot. The leaves are often coated in fine hairs, making them look like they've been dusted with flour. The stems are reddish and angular in cross-section. The flowers are inconspicuous, growing in clusters like broccoli florets.

Goosefoot is an extremely common plant, usually found as a weed in neglected places like vacant lots and roadsides. Seedlings emerge in early spring as temperatures begin to warm, growing rapidly over the summer when you can harvest its leaves and stems.

- **Nutritional Benefits:** Goosefoot ise rich in vitamins A, C, and K, calcium, iron, magnesium, and protein. The leaves can be eaten raw in salads or cooked. Its black seeds are also edible and can be used like quinoa (*C. quinoa*), a close relative.

- **Potential Look-Alikes:** Amaranths (*Amaranthus* spp.) grow in similar habitats and often have a similar overall form, but their leaves lack serrated edges, and their flowers are enclosed in spiky bracts.

- **Poisonous Counterparts:** None.

Watercress *(Nasturtium officinale)*

Watercress has compound leaves (smaller leaves on a stem) with oval leaflets.[27]

Watercress has compound leaves (smaller leaves on a stem) with oval leaflets. Each leaflet is round with smooth edges. The stems are hollow, which helps the plant float in water. Small, white, four-petaled flowers grow in clusters at the stem's tips.

This vegetable prefers clean, running water and is typically found in shallow streams. It thrives in cool, nutrient-rich water. You can collect it in late spring or early summer when it's rapidly growing. It's not a winter plant, but if the weather is not too cold in your area, you can find it in winter, too.

- **Nutritional Benefits:** You can get a lot of vitamins A, C, and K from watercress. It is essentially a vegetable containing calcium and iron. You can eat it raw or lightly cooked.

- **Potential Look-Alikes:** If you come across a plant that looks like watercress but is nowhere near water, it's probably pepperweed (*Lepidium* spp.) or bittercress (*Cardamine* spp.), both found in more terrestrial habitats and both edible. Fool's watercress (*Apium nodiflorum*) looks like watercress and grows in water. It is not toxic to humans – and many say it is a good source of antioxidants and inflammatory compounds, making it a great ingredient for boosting overall health. Its leaves are more finely divided than watercress.

- **Poisonous Counterparts:** While there are no specific toxic look-alikes for watercress, always be aware of the water surrounding it: watercress can take up pollutants from the water in which it is growing, so never harvest from dirty or polluted streams, and only harvest the parts that are growing out of the water, as the submerged parts may harbor bacteria or parasites.

Edible Flowers

Elderflower *(Sambucus cerulea)*

Elderflower belongs to the Sambucus plant family and is small and white with five petals.[38]

Blue elder (*Sambucus cerulea*) is a fast-growing shrub closely related to the European elder, which has been revered both for its medicinal uses and the flavor of its flowers and berries. Like other elders, blue elder thrives in moist, disturbed habitats: fencerows, roadsides, streambanks and open woods. Its leaves are opposite and compound, with 5-7 finely serrated leaflets.

Elders are perhaps most easily recognized when their large, flat-topped clusters of aromatic white flowers emerge in late spring or early summer. These develop into grape-like bunches of small, blue-black berries (discussed in a later chapter) by early fall.

- **Nutritional Benefits:** Elderflowers contain bioflavonoids, particularly quercetin, and are used to make syrups, teas, cordials, and liqueurs, most notably St. Germain. They are believed to have anti-inflammatory, antiviral, and immune-boosting properties, and surprisingly nutritious: rich in vitamin C, dietary fiber, and antioxidants. They are slightly toxic, so don't consume them raw. Cook them a little before consumption.

- **Poisonous Counterparts:** Two of the most poisonous plants in the Pacific Northwest closely resemble elderflowers. Poison hemlock (*Conium maculatum*) and water hemlock (*Cicuta douglasii*) both have white flower clusters similar to elder, as well as compound leaves that resemble elder leaves. However, the leaves of both plants are alternate rather than opposite, and more finely divided than elder leaves. Hemlocks are also biennial, and do not have woody stems like elder.

Poison hemlock.[29]

Fireweed *(Chamaenerion angustifolium)*

A sea of fireweed plants is soothing to look at, especially because of their striking lavender-pink flowers.[30]

A sea of fireweed plants is soothing to look at, especially because of their striking lavender-pink flowers. The flowers are four-petaled, with distinctive whisker-like stamens, and emerge in elongated spikes at the top of the plant. The leaves are narrow and lance-shaped, similar to willow leaves (in Europe, the plant is known as *rosebay willowherb* for this reason).

The plant can grow up to eight feet tall, and is often found in clearings and disturbed areas – especially recently burned land. Its flowers (which bloom in summer) ripen into long, slender seed pods in the autumn, splitting open at maturity to release thousands of tiny seeds, each with a silky parachute similar to a dandelion seed.

- **Nutritional Benefits:** Fireweed flowers are edible and can be used to garnish salads or made into syrups, jellies, and teas. Its shoots are high in vitamins A and C and can be eaten raw or cooked. In Russia, a tea made from the lightly fermented leaves is highly prized for its medicinal and tonic properties.

- **Potential Look-Alikes:** Annual or tall willowherb (*Epilobium brachycarpum*) is closely related to fireweed and can be mistaken for it. It can be distinguished from fireweed by its flowers, which have deeply notched petals, and its leaves, which are opposite rather than spirally arranged on the stem. Another potential lookalike is purple loosestrife (*Lythrum salicaria*), an invasive plant with bright pink flowers similar to fireweed, and a preference for disturbed habitats. Its leaves are opposite or whorled, while the flowers have five petals instead of four.

- **Poisonous Counterparts:** None.

Nootka Rose *(Rosa nutkana)*

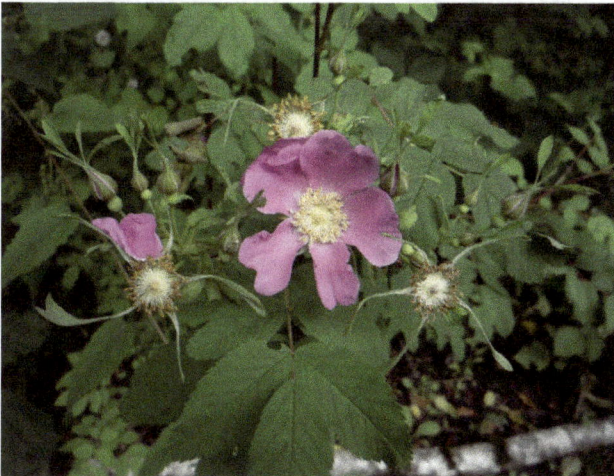

Nootka rose in bloom. Note the distinctive sepals, which are longer than the petals and persist after the petals drop off.[81]

The Nootka rose is the most common wild rose in the Pacific Northwest. The stems are sprawling and armed with prickles, while the leaves, like those of other roses, are compound, with 5 or 7 serrated leaflets. The large pink flowers have five petals and five sepals (petal-like leaves that surround the flowers), the latter distinctively elongated (often longer than the petals).

You can find Nootka roses growing on the margins of forests, in open woodlands, meadows, and along riverbanks. The flowers bloom from late spring to early summer, maturing into the distinctive fruits (hips) in the fall.

- **Nutritional Benefits:** Wild rose petals contain natural antioxidants, and rose hips are rich in vitamins A and C. You can consume them raw or use them in jellies and jams.

- **Potential Look-Alikes:** Nootka rose can be confused with other common wild rose species, including Woods' rose (*R. woodsii*) and prickly wild rose (*R. acicularis*). All species of rose are edible, but the Nootka rose can be easily distinguished by its long sepals.

Wild Berries

Huckleberries *(Vaccinium)*

Huckleberries are found throughout the Rocky Mountains range and in parts of Oregon and Washington.[a]

Huckleberries are found throughout the Rocky Mountains range and in parts of Oregon and Washington. They are round, dark blue or purple berries, somewhat similar in appearance to the closely related blueberry (*V. corymbosum* and related species) and no more than half an inch in diameter. They ripen in summer.

Huckleberry flowers are small, pink, and bell-shaped, coming to full bloom late in the spring. The plants usually grow as many-stemmed shrubs, with elliptical leaves that often turn vibrant shades of red and yellow in autumn.

- **Nutritional Benefits:** Huckleberries are excellent sources of vitamins A, C, and K and dietary fiber and antioxidants. You can eat them fresh and dried or use them in pies, jams, jellies, and syrups.

- **Potential Look-Alikes:** Blueberries are closely related to huckleberries, and grow in similar environments. Huckleberries tend to be more elongated than blueberries, which are roughly spherical – but both are edible.

- **Poisonous Counterparts:** The false huckleberry (*Rhododendron menziesii*) has similar bell-shaped flowers, a similar overall shrublike form, and often grows in the same habitats as huckleberries (forest understories). While potentially toxic in large quantities, its fruits are dry and unpalatable and unlikely to be mistaken for true huckleberries.

Salmonberries *(Rubus spectabilis)*

Salmonberries look much like the raspberries (R. idaeus) you know and love.[58]

Salmonberries are wild cousins of blackberries (*R.* subg. *Rubus*) and raspberries (*R.* subg. *Idaeobatus*); they're more closely related to the latter, although the fruits are often orange or yellow instead of red. (Fun fact: the difference between a blackberry and a raspberry isn't the color of the fruit, it's the way the fruit is attached to the stem. When you pick a blackberry, the tip of the stem comes off too; when you pick a raspberry, it detaches completely from the stem,)

Salmonberries are native to the coastal rainforests of the Northwest coast, where they grow abundantly in open woodlands (especially recently cleared forest), river banks, and roadsides. The plant itself is a sprawling, untidy shrub growing up to 9 feet high, with prickly stems and compound leaves with three serrated leaflets. The flowers, bright pink and about an inch wide, emerge in late spring, and the fruits ripen about a month later – between May and July, depending on your latitude and altitude. The ripe fruits are usually red, but sometimes yellow or orange. If you're unsure whether a berry is ripe, give it a gentle tug: ripe salmonberries will pull cleanly and easily from the stem.

- **Nutritional Benefits:** Salmonberries are rich in vitamins A and C, dietary fiber, and antioxidants. They can be eaten fresh or used in jams, jellies, pies, and desserts.

- **Poisonous Counterparts:** None. The distinctive aggregate fruits of salmonberry (as well as raspberries, blackberries, dewberries, etc.) are unique to the genus, which contains no toxic species. The biggest danger salmonberries pose to foragers is their prickles – don't forget to wear gloves when harvesting!

Thimbleberries *(Rubus parviflorus)*

Thimbleberries resemble strawberries and raspberries but are flatter and softer.[a]

Thimbleberries are closely related to salmonberries and raspberries: like those species, thimbleberries pull cleanly from their stems, leaving behind the hollow, thimble-shaped fruits that give the plant its name. Thimbleberry plants can be distinguished from most other species of bramble fairly easily, as they have large, simple leaves instead of compound leaves, and their stems lack prickles. Despite their species name, which means "small-flowered", their white flowers are actually the *largest* of any species of bramble, reaching up to 2 inches wide. The flowers emerge in spring, and the berries ripen in mid- to late summer.

Like salmonberries, thimbleberries are native to the Pacific Northwest, and tend to prefer open or disturbed areas, and are particularly abundant in recently cleared or burned forest. Unlike salmonberries, which are rarely found inland, thimbleberries grow have a fairly wide range, and can be found in dry and mountainous habitats as well as moist woods.

- **Nutritional Benefits:** Thimbleberries are high in vitamins A and C, dietary fiber, and antioxidants. Eat them fresh after foraging, or use them to make jams and jellies.

- **Poisonous Counterparts:** None. (See entry for salmonberries.)

Wild Blackberries *(Rubus* subg. *Rubus)*

Blackberries look like thimbleberries, salmonberries, raspberries, and strawberries but are black in color.[35]

Although thimbleberries and salmonberries are the most common brambles in the Northwest, blackberries are also common throughout the region, both native and introduced. The most common native species is the California blackberry (*Rubus ursinus*), which grows in similar habitats to salmonberries or thimbleberries – particularly fire-scarred forests and forest edges, especially along hiking trails and utility easements.

The plant has a more vine-like growth habit than thimbleberries or salmonberries, and its stems are heavily armed with prickles. The white flowers, which bloom in April and early May, are similar in appearance to those of many other brambles but have much thinner petals. They develop into fragrant fruits that ripen in mid-summer and look a lot like small (2cm or less) supermarket blackberries. Unlike thimbleberries and salmonberries, the ripe fruits do not pull cleanly from the stem, but take the tip (called the *torus*) with them.

- **Nutritional Benefits:** Blackberries are excellent sources of vitamins C and K, dietary fiber, and antioxidants. They are low in calories and can be eaten fresh or used like other berries.

- **Potential Look-Alikes:** Himalayan blackberry (*R. armeniacus*) has similar fruits, but is larger and more robust in almost every way (especially the prickles). It is an invasive species throughout much of the Pacific Northwest, and can outcompete and replace native species like salmonberry and California blackberry.

- **Poisonous Counterparts:** None.

Nuts and Seeds

As you may have noticed, all the edibles discussed so far (except certain seeds) are only available in the spring and summer seasons. Now, you will enter the realms of fall and winter delights!

Acorns *(Quercus* sect. *Quercus)*

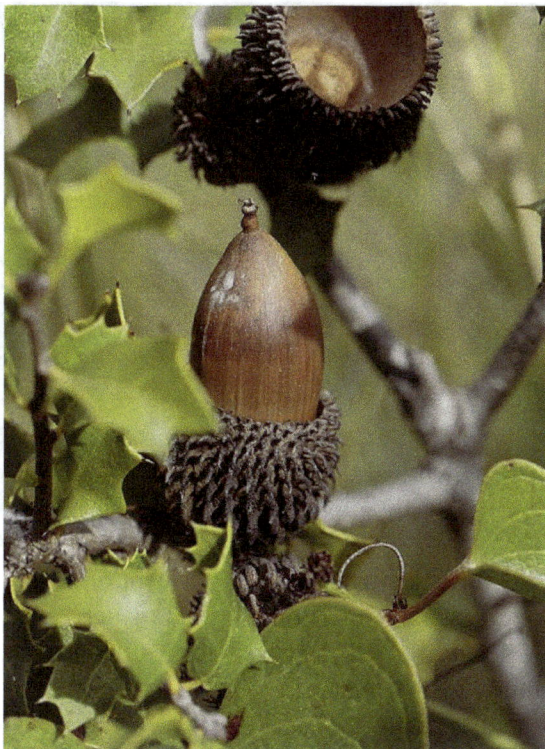

Acorns are the nuts of oak trees, enclosed in a tough, leathery shell and partially capped with a cup-like structure.[86]

Acorns are the nuts of oak trees, enclosed in a tough, leathery shell and partially capped with a cup-like structure. They usually mature and fall to the ground between September and November, and in many species they take a year and a half to ripen – meaning that the same tree may produce a lot of acorns one year and hardly any the next. Acorns, and oaks in general, contain bitter-tasting compounds called *tannins* that discourage animals from eating them, To identify oak trees, check if the leaves are deeply lobed or have smooth, wavy edges. They are broad and alternately arranged. They produce inconspicuous greenish flowers in the spring and are found in rainforests or along coasts.

- **Nutritional Benefits:** Acorns are rich in carbohydrates, fats, proteins, vitamins, and minerals. They are ground into flour and used to make porridge, bread, and other dishes.

Acorns have a unique structure and don't resemble other species in the Pacific Northwest.

Beaked Hazelnuts *(Corylus cornuta)*

Beaked hazelnut (Corylus cornuta). Note the distinctive beak-like enclosing bract. [87]

Though not as well-known as the common hazelnut (*C. avellana*), the native beaked hazel also produces edible nuts, which some foragers claim are better-tasting than their grocery store counterparts. Hazelnuts are round or oval, encased in a hard brown shell. The nut is nestled within another layer: a leafy, green husk called an involucre, which splits open when the nut matures. The involucres of beaked hazel have stiff hairs that can irritate the skin, so wear gloves when harvesting.

The trees grow along streams, in valleys and open areas. You can find them blooming with catkins and flowers in early spring, while the nuts ripen in October or November.

- **Nutritional Benefits:** Hazelnuts are abundant in healthy fats and are a good source of protein, dietary fiber, vitamins, and minerals. You can eat them raw or roasted.

- **Potential Look-Alikes:** The common hazel (*C. avellana*) is occasionally found in the Pacific Northwest as an introduced species; though much larger than beaked hazel, its nuts have a similar appearance and are also edible. Elms (*Ulmus* spp.) have similar leaves and can be mistaken for hazel, though they do not produce edible nuts.

- **Poisonous Counterparts:** None in the region; buckeyes (*Aesculus* spp.) look similar to large hazelnuts, but rarely occur in the region.

Horse chestnut.[88]

Walnuts *(Juglans* spp.*)*

Black walnuts are encased in a thick, brownish-black husk that is roughly spherical.[89]

Walnuts are related to pecans and hickories (*Carya* spp.), and like those species are more common in the eastern US. However, both the native black walnut (*J. nigra*) and the introduced English walnut (*J. regia*) can be found in the Pacific Northwest. Walnut trees are large (around 80 feet or taller) with a broad, rounded crown and compound leaves with 5-9 (English) or 15-23 (black) leaflets. The bark is dark brown to black, deeply furrowed, with a diamond-shaped pattern. The leaves emit a distinct, pungent smell when crushed. You can find both black and English walnut trees in the forests and woodlands of the Pacific Northwest, particularly in urban and suburban areas. The nuts develop in summer and mature in the fall.

- **Nutritional Benefits:** Like most other nuts, black walnuts are high in healthy fats, particularly polyunsaturated fats. They are a decent source of protein, vitamins, and minerals. Their robust, earthy flavor is used to enhance many American cuisines.

- **Potential Look-Alikes:** English walnuts would look the same as black walnuts if they had a black husk. Instead, their husk is light brown and thinner. They also have a milder flavor than black walnuts. The walnut structure is unique for its species, so you can't mistake them for existing toxic nuts.

Roots and Tubers

Camas *(Camassia)*

Camas plants produce star-shaped, purple flowers with six petals.[40]

Camas lilies are perennial wildflowers that produce underground storage organs (bulbs) shaped like eggs. The bulbs are covered in a dark, fibrous outer layer, with white flesh similar to a potato. The plants produce star-shaped purple flowers with six petals, and have long, narrow, and grass-like leaves.

Camas thrive in sunny, moist, and well-drained soils and are commonly found in seasonally wet habitats that dry out in summer, such as vernal pools and damp meadows. The plants flower in late spring, but the bulbs are best harvested in the fall when the flowers have died.

- **Nutritional Benefits:** Camas bulbs are rich in carbohydrates, particularly inulin, which converts to fructose when cooked, giving them a sweet taste.

- **Potential Look-Alikes:** A number of related species like lilies (*Lilium*) and irises (*Iris*) have similar leaves and flowers, but camas can be distinguished by its flowers, which emerge in spike-like clusters.

- **Poisonous Counterparts:** True camas can be very hard to distinguish from a number of related, but highly toxic plants often called "death camas" (*Toxicoscordion* spp.) -- which can indeed be fatal if consumed. Death camas has white flowers, while true camas has purple flowers, but otherwise the plants can be very difficult to distinguish. Thus, beginning foragers should only harvest from plants they have positively identified via the flowers.

Meadow death camas (Toxicoscordion venenosum),
one of the most common species of death camas.[a]

Burdock *(Arctium lappa)*

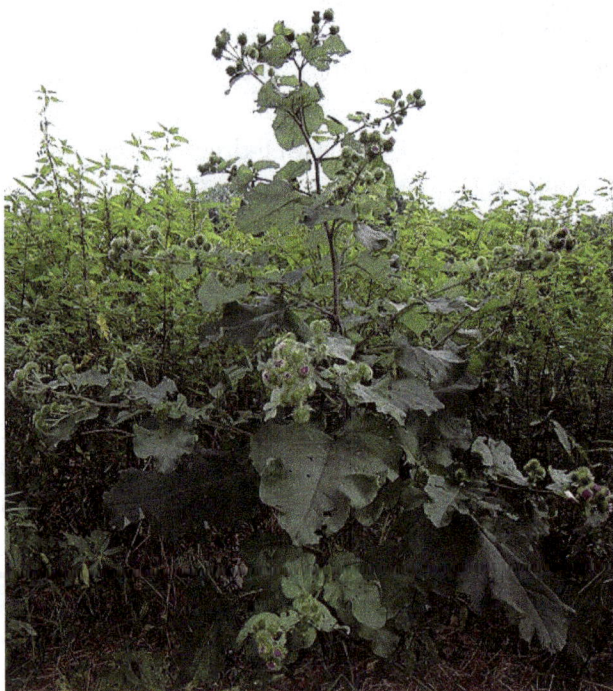

Look for large spine-like flowers (burrs) with globular heads, white to purple in color.⁴⁸

Burdock plants are common weeds of roadsides and neglected pastures, easily identified by their extremely large leaves. Like carrots (*Daucus carota*) and beets (*Beta vulgaris*) they're biennials, and like those plants they produce edible taproots in their first year. The roots are *very* long (up to three feet), slender, and brown on the outside, with white flesh inside. You can harvest them from first-year plants (i.e., plants that haven't bloomed) from late fall to early spring.

- **Nutritional Benefits:** Burdock roots have high quantities of dietary fiber, antioxidants, vitamins, and minerals. They can be eaten raw or used in tea.

- **Potential Look-Alikes:** True docks (*Rumex* spp.) have large, broad leaves and taproots similar to burdock, but never reach the size or stature of burdock, and produce inconspicuous wind-pollinated flowers that bloom each season, instead of only once.

- **Poisonous Counterparts:** Burdock has no true lookalikes, and the few plants that resemble it are safe to consume.

Wild Onions *(Allium* spp.*)*

Their flowers are white, pink, or purple with six petals.“

Dozens of species of wild onion or wild garlic can be found throughout North America, including the Pacific Northwest. Though their bulbs are not as large as their domesticated cousins, they're well worth harvesting, as are their greens (and in some species, even smaller bulblets produced in place of flowers). All species have long, narrow, leaves, which are slightly succulent and frequently tubular in cross-section, and which emit a strong onion or garlic odor when crushed. Their flowers are six-petaled, white to pink in color, and bloom in clusters at the tops of tubular flower stalks called *scapes.* Nearly all species grow best in sunny, moist habitats like stream banks, wet meadows, and river bottoms. The bulbs are best harvested in the fall and winter seasons, while the greens can be harvested year-round (if available).

Its nutritional benefits are like the camas and onions, and, as you well know, it can be used in any number of dishes.

- **Poisonous Counterparts:** Numerous related plants can resemble wild onions, including the aforementioned death camas (*Toxicoscordion* spp.). However, edible onions can be distinguished from toxic lookalikes quite easily by their distinctive odor of onions or garlic, which is produced only by plants in the genus *Allium.* Remember: if it doesn't smell like an onion, it probably isn't!

Wild Carrots *(Daucus carota)*

Their leaves are finely divided and feathery, and the flowers are white and clustered to form a dome."

Wild carrot, also commonly called Queen Anne's lace, is the direct ancestor of the carrots you're used to seeing in grocery stores. It also produces edible taproots, which look a little like those carrots but smaller and paler. The plant's leaves are finely divided and feathery, and the white flowers are borne in large clusters called *umbels*, which often have a single purple or red flower in the center. You can find them along roadsides, meadows, and other disturbed habitats. Harvest the roots from first-year plants in the fall or winter before they flower; the roots of flowering plants are fibrous and unpalatable.

- **Nutritional Benefits:** They have an abundance of vitamins A, C, and K and can be eaten raw or cooked.

- **Poisonous Counterparts:** Several other common plants have white flowers that grow in a dome-shaped cluster, including some of the most poisonous plants on the continent: poison hemlock (*Conium maculatum*) and water hemlock (*Cicuta douglasii*) are the two most common, and most dangerous. To distinguish these from wild carrot, look closely at the stems: wild carrots have hairy stems, while theirs are hairless and smooth.

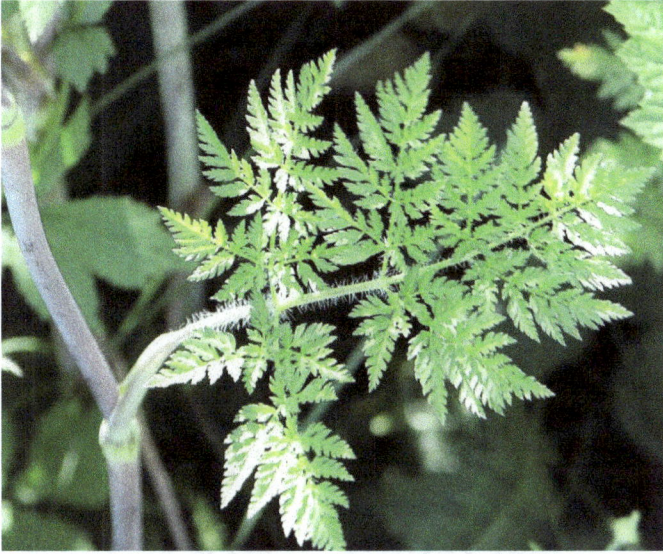

Poison hemlock.[6]

The list goes on as you cycle back from the fall and winter to spring, with an exciting growth of mushrooms in the next chapter.

Chapter 5: Mushrooms of the Pacific Northwest

Fungi are essential for the planet's health and crucial in forest ecosystems, helping to decompose dead plants and animals."

Fungi are essential for the planet's health and crucial in forest ecosystems, helping to decompose dead plants and animals. This decomposition process recycles nutrients into the soil, allowing new plants to grow. Forests will struggle to thrive without fungi because essential nutrients would not be available.

Also, fungi form symbiotic partnerships with trees. Many trees rely on fungi to help absorb water and soil nutrients. In return, the trees provide the fungi with sugars they produce through photosynthesis. This mutually beneficial relationship is essential for the forests' growth and health.

Decomposition

Fungi are primary decomposers of organic matter, like dead plants, leaves, and animals. They break down complex organic compounds like cellulose and lignin into simpler substances. This process releases essential nutrients into the soil, like carbon, nitrogen, and phosphorus, which plants need to grow.

Nutrient Cycling

Fungi facilitate the recycling of nutrients from the decomposing organic matter. This process ensures nutrients are continuously made available to living plants. Without fungi, dead organic material would accumulate, and nutrients would remain locked in unusable forms, leading to a nutrient deficit for living plants.

Mycorrhizal Associations

Many fungi form symbiotic relationships with plants, particularly trees, through structures known as mycorrhizae. In this mutualistic relationship, the fungal mycelium (the network of hyphae) extends into the soil, increasing the surface area for water and nutrient absorption. The tree, in turn, provides the fungus with carbohydrates produced through photosynthesis. There are two main mycorrhizae:

Ectomycorrhizae

These form a sheath around the roots and penetrate the root cortex cells without invading them. They are common in temperate forest trees like pines, oaks, and birches.

Arbuscular Mycorrhizae

These penetrate the root cells and are found in various plants, including many forest species. They help the absorption of phosphorus and other micronutrients.

Species Diversity

Forest ecosystems host diverse fungal species, each adapted to specific ecological niches. This diversity includes visible mushrooms, toadstools, and a vast array of microscopic fungi living in the soil, on tree bark, and within decaying wood.

Fungi also interact with various organisms in the forest besides living in symbiosis with plants. They can be mutualists, pathogens, or decomposers. Some fungi form lichens associated with algae or cyanobacteria, contributing to soil formation by breaking down rocks.

Plant Health and Growth

Mycorrhizal fungi enhance plant health by improving nutrient uptake, water absorption, and resistance to pathogens. They can help plants tolerate environmental stressors like drought and soil salinity.

Fungal Networks and Communication

Wood Wide Web

Fungi create extensive underground networks, called the *Wood Wide Web*, which connect individual plants and trees. These networks allow the transfer of nutrients, water, and chemical signals between plants. Trees can share resources through these networks, transferring nutrients to the trees needing them the most. This underground network works like a charm for the plants, enhancing the resilience and stability of the forest community.

Chemical Signaling

Fungi can detect and respond to environmental changes. They release chemicals that signal to plants about pathogens or stress, prompting the plants to activate their defense mechanisms.

Ecological Balance and Sustainability

Population Control

Fungi regulate various organisms' populations in the forest by acting as natural pathogens to some plants and animals. This population control prevents certain species from dominating the ecosystem, maintaining biodiversity and ecological balance.

Habitat Creation

Fungi create habitats for various organisms by decomposing dead trees and other organic matter. Rotting logs and leaf litter provides homes for insects, small mammals, and other fungi, further enriching the ecosystem's biodiversity.

Understanding the diversity and complexity of fungi helps you appreciate their vital role in nature. There are countless fungi species, each with unique functions and characteristics. They range from the familiar mushrooms on the forest floor to microscopic fungi in the soil. Each fungus contributes specifically to the balance and health of forest ecosystems.

Mushroom Anatomy

Understanding mushroom anatomy and terminology is crucial if you want to identify mushrooms accurately. This knowledge is critical if you forage wild mushrooms, as some can be poisonous and potentially deadly. Here is a basic overview of mushroom anatomy and essential terms to help you get started:

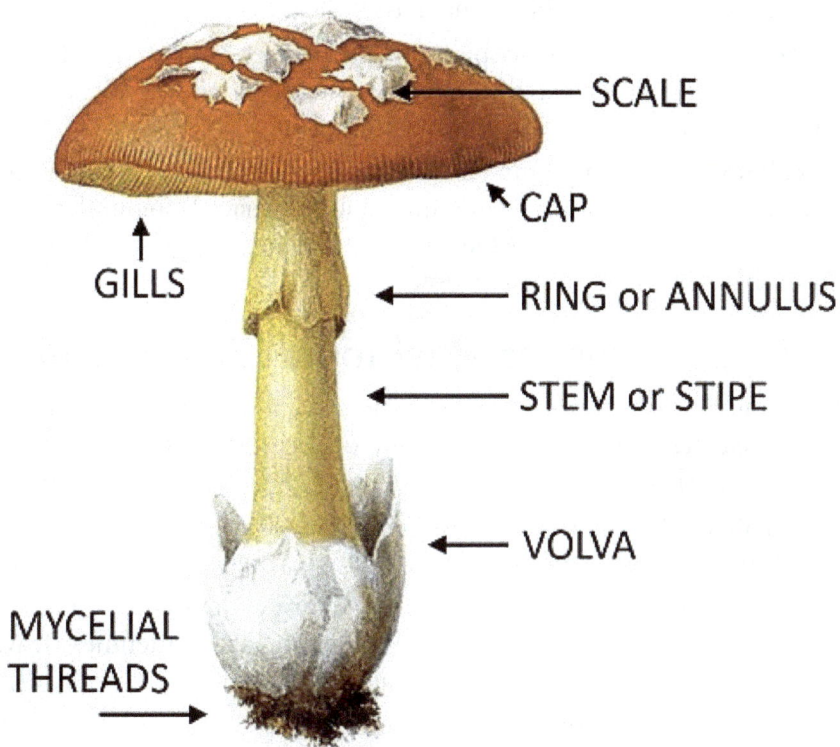

Understanding mushroom anatomy and terminology is crucial if you want to identify mushrooms accurately.[7]

Cap (Pileus): The cap is the top part of the mushroom, often umbrella-shaped. It can come in various colors, shapes, and sizes. The surface may be smooth, scaly, or sticky.

Gills (Lamellae): Located on the underside of the cap, gills are thin, blade-like structures. They produce spores, which are the reproductive units of the mushroom. The color and spacing of gills are important for identification.

Stem (Stipe): The stem supports the cap and elevates it above the ground. Its characteristics, like its thickness, length, and ring, will identify the mushroom.

Ring (Annulus): This is a ring-like structure found on the stem, usually a remnant of the partial veil covering immature mushrooms' gills. Not all mushrooms have a ring.

Volva: The volva is a cup-like structure at the base of the stem, a remnant of the universal veil that encloses the mushroom when it is young. The presence and appearance of a volva are essential for identifying certain species, like Amanitas.

Spores: Spores are microscopic reproductive cells released by the gills, pores, or other structures. Spore color can be a critical identification feature often determined by making a spore print.

Mycelium: The mycelium is the vegetative part of the fungus, comprising a network of fine white filaments (hyphae) living in the soil or wood. It is not usually visible when foraging but is vital for the mushroom's growth and reproduction.

Critical Terms for Mushroom Identification

Spore Print: A spore print is made by placing the cap gills on paper or glass and leaving it overnight. The color of the spores that fall can help identify the mushroom.

Partial Veil: This membrane covers the gills of a young mushroom. As the mushroom matures, the veil breaks, often leaving a ring on the stem.

Universal Veil: The membrane entirely encloses immature mushrooms. As the mushroom grows, it breaks, sometimes leaving fragments at the base (volva) or on the cap.

Pores: Some mushrooms, like boletes, have pores instead of gills. Pores are small holes on the underside of the cap where spores are released.

Scales: These are rough, often raised patches on the cap or stem. They can be remnants of the universal veil or the mushroom's natural features.

Importance of Accurate Identification

Accurate identification of mushrooms is crucial, especially if you plan to forage and consume wild mushrooms. Many edible mushrooms have toxic look-alikes that can cause severe illness or death if ingested. Here are reasons caution and accurate identification are essential:

Avoiding Poisoning: Some mushrooms contain potent toxins, causing severe symptoms or are fatal. For example, Amanita phalloides (the death cap) looks similar to some edible mushrooms but contains deadly toxins.

Health Risks: Even non-lethal poisonous mushrooms can cause gastrointestinal distress, allergic reactions, or long-term health issues. Accurate identification prevents these risks.

Environmental Impact: Some mushrooms are critical in nutrient cycling and plant health. Harvesting the wrong mushrooms can disturb local ecosystems.

Legal Considerations: Foraging for certain wild mushrooms is regulated or restricted in some areas to protect endangered species and habitats. Knowing which mushrooms are safe and legal to harvest is essential.

Understanding mushroom anatomy and terminology lays the foundation for accurate identification and safe foraging. Always exercise caution when collecting wild mushrooms, as many edible species have dangerous look-alikes. Consult experienced foragers, mycologists, or reliable resources if in doubt, and consider participating in local mushroom hunting groups to improve your skills and knowledge.

Accurate identification is essential, especially when foraging for edible mushrooms, as many have toxic look-alikes."

Identifying mushrooms can be a rewarding yet challenging activity. Accurate identification is essential, especially when foraging for edible mushrooms, as many have toxic look-alikes. Here are some tips and techniques for distinguishing between edible, inedible, and poisonous species, along with using multiple verification sources.

Tips for Mushroom Identification

Observe the Environment

Note the habitat where the mushroom grows. Certain species prefer different environments (e.g., forests, grasslands, or near specific trees). For example, chanterelles *(Cantharellus cibarius)* are often found in deciduous forests. In contrast, morels *(Morchella spp.)* can be found in wooded areas or near dead elm trees.

Examine the Cap: Look at the cap's shape, color, texture, and size. For example, the edible hen of the woods *(Grifola frondosa)* has a distinctive rosette shape with overlapping, grayish-brown caps.

Check the Gills or Pores: Identify if the mushroom has gills, pores, or other spore-producing surfaces. Note their color, attachment to the stem, and spacing. Edible mushrooms like the common button mushroom *(Agaricus bisporus)* have free gills unattached to the stem. Poisonous species like the death cap *(Amanita phalloides)* have white, free gills.

Examine the Stem: Note the stem's size, color, texture, and presence of rings or volvas. The edible shiitake *(Lentinula edodes)* has a rugged, fibrous stem. In contrast, the highly poisonous destroying *angel (Amanita bisporigera)* has a smooth, white stem with a prominent volva at the base.

Make a Spore Print: Collect spore prints to determine the spore color. It could be a key identifying feature. For example, the spore print of the edible oyster mushroom *(Pleurotus ostreatus)* is white to lilac-gray. In contrast, the spore print of the poisonous false parasol *(Chlorophyllum molybdites)* is green.

Smell and Taste (with Caution): Some mushrooms have distinctive smells or tastes, but only taste a mushroom if you are confident it is non-toxic. For instance, the edible black trumpet *(Craterellus cornucopioides)* has a pleasant, fruity smell, while the inedible sulfur tuft *(Hypholoma fasciculare)* smells bitter and unpleasant.

Techniques for Distinguishing Mushrooms

Look-Alike Comparisons

Compare the mushroom with known species, noting key differences in shape, size, color, texture, smell, and whether they grow in clusters or individually. For instance, the edible meadow mushroom *(Agaricus campestris)* can be confused with the toxic yellow-staining mushroom *(Agaricus xanthodermus),* which turns yellow when bruised.

Online Resources

Refer to reliable field guides with detailed descriptions and photos or reputable online databases and identification apps. These platforms allow you to compare your finds with a vast database of images and descriptions.

Field Guides:

- *National Audubon Society Field Guide to North American Mushrooms* – National Audubon Society.
- *Peterson Field Guide to Mushrooms of North America, Second Edition (Peterson Field Guides)* – Karl B. McKnight, Joseph R. Rohrer, et al.
- *Mushrooms: How to Identify and Gather Wild Mushrooms and Other Fungi* – DK Publishing.

Websites:

- https://www.mushroom.world/mushrooms/list
- https://www.first-nature.com/fungi/index.php
- https://www.mushroomexpert.com/

Identification Apps:

- Champignouf
- Shroomid
- iNaturalist

Local Mycological Societies

Join local mycological societies or clubs. These groups often organize forays, conduct identification workshops, and access experts. Participating in group activities enhances your learning and ensures safer foraging.

Use the following websites to find a mycological society near you:

- https://namyco.org/clubs/
- https://msafungi.org/

Examples

Edible Mushrooms

- **Chanterelle** *(Cantharellus cibarius)*: Bright yellow to orange, with ridged gills and a fruity smell

- **Morel** *(Morchella spp.)*: Honeycomb-like cap with pits, ridges, and a hollow stem

- **Porcini** *(Boletus edulis)*: Brown, convex cap with a thick, white stalk and a pleasant nutty smell

Inedible Mushrooms

- **False Morel** *(Gyromitra spp.)*: Wrinkled, irregular cap, toxic if not prepared correctly

- **Red Cracking Bolete** *(Xerocomellus chrysenteron)*: Red-brown cap with a cracked surface, inedible due to poor taste and texture

Poisonous Mushrooms

- **Death Cap** *(Amanita phalloides)*: Greenish cap, white gills, volva at the base, and deadly toxic

Death cap.[40]

- **Destroying Angel** *(Amanita bisporigera)*: Pure white mushroom, volva at the base, and deadly toxic

Destroying Angel.[50]

- **Jack O'Lantern** *(Omphalotus illudens):* Bright orange gills that glow in the dark and cause severe gastrointestinal distress

Jack O'Lantern.[51]

Importance of Using Multiple Sources for Verification

Using multiple sources like cross-referencing and consulting mycologists for expert opinion is necessary to keep your foraging adventures safe and nutritious. The sole purpose of using multiple references is to prevent misidentification. Each guide or source may emphasize different distinguishing features of a mushroom, like cap shape, spore color, or habitat. However, it's better to be safe than sorry.

Although you will be using multiple sources, take detailed photos of the mushroom's habitat, including different angles and critical features. This documentation can help experts assist you in identification. The documentation can be your reference for the mushroom's exact identification for your upcoming foraging expeditions.

Using multiple sources provides a richer, more detailed understanding of mushrooms. Different guides offer varying insights into a mushroom's ecological role, growth patterns, and habitats, helping you make informed decisions. Furthermore, while one source might focus on the mushroom's culinary uses, another might provide details on its medicinal properties or specific preparation methods, giving a fuller picture of the mushroom's potential value.

Furthermore, mushrooms that appear similar can belong to different species in various regions. Consulting regional guides alongside general ones ensures identification considers local species variations. Seasonal changes can affect a mushroom's appearance, and multiple sources will provide insights into how mushrooms may look at different times of the year, enhancing the identification accuracy.

Using multiple sources for verification can improve your mushroom identification skills and enable you to forage more safely. Remember, do not consume the mushroom when in doubt. Safety should always be your top priority.

Besides proper identification, responsible foraging practices should be used to help protect the environment and ensure the sustainability of mushroom populations. Here are essential safety tips and guidelines for responsible foraging:

Safety Considerations

Identification: Before consuming a wild mushroom, you must know its identification. Misidentifying a mushroom can lead to severe illness or death.

Key Features: Learn to recognize features like cap shape, gill attachment, spore print color, and rings or volvas.

Examples of Dangerous Look-Alikes

Chanterelle *(Cantharellus cibarius)* is an edible mushroom but has a very toxic look-alike called Jack O'Lantern *(Omphalotus illudens)*. Both are orange, but Jack O'Lantern has true gills and glows faintly in the dark. Chanterelles have ridges and do not glow.

Likewise, the meadow mushroom *(Agaricus campestris)* resembles the poisonous yellow-staining mushroom *(Agaricus xanthodermus)*. Both are white, but the yellow-staining mushroom turns yellow when bruised and smells unpleasant.

Avoid Toxic Mushrooms

- **Death Cap** *(Amanita phalloides)*. Greenish cap, white gills, with a volva at the base

- **Destroying Angel** *(Amanita bisporigera)*. Pure white, with a volva at the base

- **False Parasol** *(Chlorophyllum molybdites)*. Green spore print, standard in lawns and meadows

Even experienced foragers can make mistakes. When encountering a new or unfamiliar species, consult multiple sources and experts before consuming.

Responsible Foraging Practices

Minimize Environmental Impact

Be mindful of your surroundings and avoid disturbing the habitat. Stick to established trails and minimize trampling vegetation. Furthermore, only take what you need and leave some mushrooms behind to allow for natural reproduction and ecosystem balance.

Respect Local Regulations

Check for required permits and follow local foraging regulations. Some areas may have restrictions to protect endangered species or sensitive habitats.

Harvesting Techniques

Gently cut or twist mushrooms at the base to minimize damage to the mycelium. This underground network supports mushroom growth. Collect only a few of the mushrooms in one area to avoid overharvesting. Leave enough for wildlife and future growth.

Spread Knowledge

Share your knowledge about safe and sustainable foraging practices. Encourage new foragers to learn from multiple reliable sources. Join local mycological societies to stay informed about the latest research, regulations, and best practices.

Environmental Stewardship

Be aware of changes in the ecosystem that might affect mushroom populations, like pollution, deforestation, or climate change. You can contribute to citizen science projects and report your findings to local mycological societies. This data helps track the health of mushroom populations and ecosystems.

Mushrooms of the Pacific Northwest

The Pacific Northwest is a rich region for mushroom foraging, brimming with various edible species. Below are detailed profiles of common edible mushrooms in this area, their habitats, and tips for sustainable harvesting.

Chanterelle *(cantharellus cibarius)*

Chanterelles are easily recognized by their golden yellow to orange color and funnel-shaped caps.[53]

Chanterelles are easily recognized by their golden yellow to orange color and funnel-shaped caps. In place of gills, they have ridged, forking folds on the underside of the cap that run down the stem.

Habitat: Chanterelles grow in coniferous and deciduous forests, often under Douglas fir, hemlock, or oak trees. They prefer mossy, moist areas from late summer to early winter.

Sustainable Harvesting Tips

1. Harvest by cutting the mushroom at the base, leaving the mycelium intact.
2. Avoid Overharvesting. Only take what you need and leave smaller mushrooms to mature.
3. Use a knife to avoid disturbing the forest floor.

Morels *(Morchella spp.)*

Morels have a distinctive honeycomb appearance with a conical cap covered in pits and ridges.[58]

Morels have distinctive honeycombed caps, which lack gills and are fully attached to the hollow stems. They range in color from tan to dark brown.

Habitat: Morels are typically found in moist, sandy soils in forested areas, especially around dead or dying elm, ash, and apple trees. They often appear in the spring after rain.

Sustainable Harvesting Tips

1. Gently twist or cut morels at the base to protect the body.
2. Avoid picking all the morels in one area to allow for future growth.
3. Be mindful of the habitat and minimize trampling.

Lobster Mushrooms *(Hypomyces lactifluorum)*

Lobster mushrooms are parasitic fungi that engulf other mushrooms, typically russulas or Lactarius, turning them reddish or orange.[54]

Lobster mushrooms are parasitic fungi that engulf other mushrooms, typically russulas or *Lactarius* species, turning them reddish or orange. The texture is dense, and the taste is like seafood.

Habitat: Found in mixed hardwood and conifer forests, often near hemlock and pine trees. They grow from late summer to fall.

Sustainable Harvesting Tips

1. Harvest by cutting at the base, leaving some behind to spore.
2. Ensure you harvest in a non-contaminated area to avoid toxic substances.

Oyster Mushrooms *(Pleurotus ostreatus)*

Oyster mushrooms have broad, fan-shaped caps, usually white to light brown.[55]

Oyster mushrooms have broad, fan-shaped caps, usually white to light brown. They have decurrent gills running down a short or absent stem.

Habitat: They grow on decaying hardwood logs and stumps, mainly beech and oak. They can be found year-round, particularly in more relaxed, moist conditions.

Sustainable Harvesting Tips

1. Cut the mushrooms close to the wood to leave the mycelium intact.

2. Harvest selectively, allowing some clusters to continue growing.

3. Avoid collecting in polluted areas.

Lion's Mane *(Hericium erinaceus)*

Lion's Mane mushrooms have a unique appearance, with long, white, cascading spines resembling a lion's manes.[56]

Lion's Mane mushrooms have a unique appearance, with long, white, cascading spines resembling hair or a lion's mane. They are known for their crab- or lobster-like flavor.

Habitat: Found on hardwood trees, mainly oak, beech, and maple. They grow from late summer to early winter.

Sustainable Harvesting Tips

1. Cut the mushroom at the base to avoid damaging the tree and the mycelium.
2. Take only mature specimens and leave younger ones to grow.
3. Do not harvest from living trees in protected areas.

Porcini *(Boletus edulis)*

Porcini mushrooms have large, brown, convex caps and thick, white stems."

Porcini mushrooms have large, brown, convex caps and thick, white stems covered with

net-like ridges. The underside of the cap features spongy pores rather than gills.

Habitat: Typically found in coniferous and deciduous forests, particularly under pine, spruce, and fir trees. They appear in late summer to fall.

Sustainable Harvesting Tips

1. Harvest, twist, or cut the stem carefully to avoid disturbing the soil.
2. Avoid picking young porcini to allow them to mature.
3. Stay within one area to ensure future growth.

Matsutake *(Tricholoma matsutake)*

Matsutake mushrooms have a white to brownish cap with a distinctive spicy aroma.[58]

Matsutake mushrooms have a white to brownish cap with a distinctive spicy aroma. They have thick, white stems with a ring near the top and gills that turn brown as they age.

Habitat: Found in coniferous forests, especially under pine trees. They grow in sandy, well-drained soils from late summer to fall.

Sustainable Harvesting Tips

1. Carefully dig around the base to avoid damaging the mycelium.
2. Only mature specimens are harvested, and younger ones are left to grow.
3. Practice minimal impact foraging to protect the ecosystem.

Cauliflower Mushrooms *(Sparassis crispa)*

Cauliflower mushrooms have a unique, frilly appearance resembling a cauliflower head.[59]

Cauliflower mushrooms have a unique, frilly appearance resembling a cauliflower head. They are white to yellowish and have a mild, nutty flavor.

Habitat: Found at the base of coniferous trees, mainly pines and firs. They grow from late summer to fall.

Sustainable Harvesting Tips

1. Cut the mushroom at the base, leaving part of it behind to promote regrowth.
2. Only harvest moderately from one location.
3. Handle gently to avoid damaging the delicate fronds.

Chicken-of-the-Woods *(Laetiporus sulphureus)*

Chicken-of-the-Woods mushrooms have bright yellow to orange shelves with a soft, fleshy texture.[60]

Chicken-of-the-Woods mushrooms have bright yellow to orange shelves with a soft, fleshy texture. They grow in overlapping clusters and have a chicken-like flavor when cooked.

Habitat: Found on decaying hardwood trees, like oak, cherry, and chestnut. They appear from late spring to fall.

Sustainable Harvesting Tips

1. Cut the outer edges of the clusters, leaving the base attached to the tree.
2. Harvest only from trees that are not in protected areas.
3. Avoid overharvesting to ensure the population can sustain itself.

General Tips for Sustainable Foraging

- Learn about local regulations and guidelines for foraging in your area. Some regions may have specific rules to protect species or habitats.

- Only take what you need and leave enough mushrooms behind for natural reproduction and ecological balance.

- Be mindful of the environment. Avoid trampling vegetation and disturbing wildlife. Stick to established paths when possible.

- Always leave some mushrooms to ensure they can spore and propagate future growth.

- Always seek permission before foraging on private land and follow posted signs or regulations in public areas.

This chapter was about the mushrooms in the Pacific Northwest. While these nutritious edibles look easy to forage, the key is to stay safe. Avoiding adverse reactions after consumption is only possible through adequate identification. Always start with different parts like the cap, stem, gills, volva, etc., one at a time, so you know the differentiating factors between the edible and toxic mushroom varieties. It's better to attend mushroom identification classes or join forays to get hands-on experience with identification, safe foraging, and handling if you are a beginner.

Chapter 6: Cooking Wild Edibles: 17 Easy Recipes

Living in the Pacific Northwest enables you to forage various plants and mushrooms to cook healthy and tasty dishes for yourself and your family. This chapter includes easy recipes and cooking tips to prepare creative meals.

Cooking Tips

Follow these cooking tips before preparing your recipes:

- Read the entire recipe before cooking

- Get creative and experiment with different ingredients

- Don't improvise while baking

- Pay attention to the ingredients' texture and consistency while cooking

- Rinse the plants thoroughly before cooking and remove the roots, dirt, insects, and other parts you won't use

- Store the plants in the freezer or refrigerator after cleaning them to preserve their freshness and flavor

- Start cooking with familiar plants and only incorporate small quantities into your recipes until you get used to their taste and impact on your health since some plants have allergenic properties

- Combine wild edible plants with ingredients that highlight their flavor
- Wild edible plants can be cooked using various methods, such as blanching, pickling, and sautéing

Chanterelle Risotto

Pairing chanterelle mushrooms with corn and rice will result in a delicious dish rich in flavor.[61]

Chanterelle mushrooms have a unique and strong flavor and are a great addition to any recipe. Pairing them with corn and rice will result in a delicious dish rich in flavor.

Ingredients:

- ½ pound of diced chanterelle mushrooms
- 2 cups of carnaroli or arborio risotto rice
- 1 cup of sweet corn kernels
- 4 tablespoons of divided butter
- 6 cups of chicken stock
- 2 cloves of minced garlic
- 1 teaspoon of dried thyme
- ½ cup of minced onion or 1 minced shallot
- ¼ cup of grated parmesan or pecorino cheese
- ½ cup of white wine
- Salt

Instructions:

1. Put the chicken stock in a large pot and let it simmer.
2. Put two tablespoons of the butter in another pot and heat on the stove until it melts.
3. Add the minced onion or shallot to the butter and cook over medium heat for four minutes or until it softens.
4. Add salt while the onion is cooking.
5. Add the diced chanterelles and the garlic, increase the heat to medium-high, and cook for five minutes while stirring.
6. Add the rice and cook for two minutes until it turns translucent. Stir frequently.
7. Add the thyme and the white wine.
8. The ingredients should sputter. Keep stirring until the rice absorbs the wine.
9. Next, add one or two ladles of the hot stock one at a time and stir frequently.
10. Let the ingredients cook on steady heat until they boil and bubble.
11. Keep pouring in the stock while stirring and let them cook for 20 minutes or until the rice feels tender.
12. Once the rice is cooked, add the two tablespoons of butter, grated cheese, and corn.
13. Add more stock to make it soupier. (Add water if you run out of stock).
14. Season with salt to taste and serve hot.

Morel Stuffed Chicken Breast

The morel stuffed chicken breast recipe is unlike any chicken dish you have tasted. The mushrooms and herbs give it a unique and mouthwatering taste.

Ingredients:

- 4 skinless and boneless chicken breasts
- 1 cup of chopped morel mushrooms
- 2 tablespoons of olive oil
- 2 tablespoons of chopped fresh thyme

- ¼ cup of chopped fresh parsley
- 2 cloves of minced garlic
- Salt and pepper for seasoning

Instructions:

1. Preheat the oven to 375 °F.
2. Put the chopped thyme, chopped parsley, minced garlic, chopped morel mushrooms, and salt and pepper in a mixing bowl and combine.
3. Cut a small pocket into each chicken breast for the stuffing.
4. Stuff with the mushroom mixture and secure it with toothpicks.
5. Put the olive oil in an oven-safe skillet and heat over medium-high heat.
6. Cook each side of the stuffed chicken breast for three minutes or until they turn golden brown.
7. Put the skillet in the oven and let it bake for 30 minutes.
8. Remove from the oven, let it sit for five minutes, and serve.

Salmonberry Sorbet

This refreshing and fruity sorbet will keep you cool on hot summer days."

This refreshing and fruity sorbet will keep you cool on hot summer days. You won't get enough of it, thanks to its sweet salmonberry flavor.

Ingredients:

- 2 cups of salmonberries
- ½ lemon, juiced
- ¾ cup of granulated sugar

Instructions:

1. Pour a cup of water into a large pan and add the sugar.
2. Cook over medium heat for two minutes or until the sugar is dissolved.
3. Increase the heat to medium-high heat and boil the water for three minutes or until it thickens like syrup.
4. Pour the liquid into a heat-proof jug, add the lemon juice, and stir.
5. Leave it for a few minutes to cool.
6. Place the salmonberries in a food processor and blend until they become a puree-like texture.
7. Pour the blended salmonberries into a large bowl using a sieve. Press on the salmonberries through the sieve to squeeze as much juice as possible.
8. After the syrup cools down, pour it over the bowl with the sieve. Throw away the seeds.
9. Stir to combine the syrup with the juice
10. Pour into a freezer-proof container and seal tightly.
11. Leave it in the freezer for two hours.
12. Remove from the freezer and break up the ice crystals with a fork to smoothen the mixture.
13. Return it to the freezer for another two hours.
14. Remove from the freezer and break up the ice crystals again.
15. Repeat three times every hour until the sorbet is set.
16. Leave the sorbet in the freezer and take it out 15 minutes before serving to allow it to soften so you can scoop it easily.

Hazelnut-Crusted Salmon

Prepare this crunchy dish with vegetables and rice and serve it for a delicious and healthy lunch for you and your family.

Ingredients:

- 2 pounds of salmon, sliced into 4 pieces
- ½ cup of hazelnuts
- 3 tablespoons of olive oil
- 2 tablespoons of lemon juice
- ¼ cup of panko bread crumbs
- 1 tablespoon of honey
- ¼ teaspoon of pepper
- 1 teaspoon of salt

Instructions:

1. Preheat the oven to 375° F.
2. Place parchment paper on a large sheet pan.
3. Put the salmon pieces on top.
4. In a small bowl, whisk the lemon juice and honey, and then drizzle onto the salmon.
5. In a food processor, grind the hazelnuts until they are a fine powder.
6. Next, with the hazelnut powder, add in the pepper, salt, olive oil, breadcrumbs and panko and mix. You need to make sure it's just wet enough so that it sticks to the salmon.
7. Bake the salmon pieces in the preheated oven for 25 minutes or until the hazelnut crust turns golden brown and the salmon is cooked.
8. Serve hot.

Nettle and Potato Soup

This soup is the perfect appetizer for an outdoor spring meal with family and friends.[68]

This soup is the perfect appetizer for an outdoor spring meal with family and friends. The nettle enhances the taste and makes this soup stand out from any you have tasted.

Ingredients:

- 1 pound of nettles
- 1 pound of chopped potatoes
- 6 cups of chicken broth
- 1 peeled and diced onion
- 2 chopped cloves garlic
- 2 tablespoons of butter or olive oil
- ½ teaspoon of black pepper
- 2 teaspoons of salt

Instructions:

1. Use tongs or wear rubber gloves when handling raw nettles.
2. Put the nettles in a large bowl, cover them with water, and let them soak for a few seconds. With the gloves and tongs, remove and discard the dirty water.

3. Repeat until the nettles are clean.

4. Put the oil or butter in a Dutch oven and leave it on medium heat.

5. Add the onion and sauté for five minutes or until the onions turn golden.

6. Add the garlic and stir for 30 seconds.

7. Add the nettles and potatoes and stir for one minute.

8. Stir in the broth and add the salt and pepper.

9. Increase the heat to boil.

10. Cover the Dutch oven and lower the heat to simmer for 30 minutes or until the potatoes are tender.

11. Blend to puree the soup.

12. Serve hot.

Elderflower Lemonade

Cool yourself with this refreshing lemonade and enjoy the taste of honey and elderflowers.

Ingredients:

- 15 heads of elderflowers (1 cup)
- Zest of 4 lemons
- 1 cup of honey
- 1 ½ cups of lemon juice
- 8 cups of water
- 4 elderflower blossoms and 2 lemon slices for garnish

Instructions:

1. Remove the stems from the elderflowers.

2. Put the elderflower heads, lemon zest, and honey in a heat-proof container.

3. Heat one cup of water to below boiling.

4. Pour the heated water over the elderflowers and berry mixture and stir to mix.

5. Cover the mixture with a cloth and let it steep for two hours.

6. After the mixture is steeped, pour it into a large container or pitcher with a sieve.

7. Pour in the lemon juice and remaining water and stir.

8. Garnish with the elderflower blossoms and lemon slices and serve cold.

9. Store the remaining lemonade in a sealed container and keep it in the refrigerator for two to three days.

Wild Mushroom Tart

You can have this dish for breakfast, lunch, or dinner.[6]

You can have this dish for breakfast, lunch, or dinner. Store the leftovers in the fridge, warm it in the microwave, and eat it the next day. It will still taste fresh.

Crust Ingredients:

- 2 tablespoons of ice water
- ¾ cup of cold unsalted butter, sliced into small cubes
- ¼ teaspoon of salt
- 2 cups of unbleached all-purpose flour

Filling Ingredients:

- 1 pound of shallots
- ¼ cup of heavy cream
- 3 tablespoons of chives
- ¾ cup of divided parmesan cheese
- ¾ cup of ricotta cheese
- 1 large egg
- 1 ½ pounds of wild mushrooms
- 2 tablespoons of butter
- ½ teaspoon of ground black pepper, divided
- 1 ½ teaspoons of salt, divided
- 2 tablespoons of balsamic vinegar
- 3 tablespoons of olive oil, divided
- Microgreens for garnish
- Fresh thyme for garnish

Instructions:

1. Preheat the oven to 350° F.
2. Prepare the dough by putting the salt and flour in a food processor and pulsing.
3. Add the butter and pulse again until it has an oatmeal texture.
4. Add the ice water and pulse twice. The dough should clump together.
5. Put the flour on a wooden board and roll it into a ball.
6. Wrap it in plastic paper and leave it in the refrigerator for 30 minutes.
7. While the dough chills in the refrigerator, peel and remove the shallot's root ends.
8. Cut them into quarters and put them in a small sheet pan.
9. Add two tablespoons of olive oil, ¼ teaspoon of pepper, 1 teaspoon of salt, and the vinegar.
10. Roast in the preheated oven for 45 minutes or until the onions soften and change color.

11. Remove it from the oven and let it sit and cool.

12. While the onions are in the oven, cook the mushrooms.

13. Put the butter in a pan and melt over medium heat.

14. Add the mushrooms and the remaining salt and pepper.

15. Sautee for ten minutes or until they turn golden and remove from the stove.

16. After the dough is chilled, spread it on a lightly floured surface to a 12-inch circle.

17. Slowly place the rolled dough in a tart ring and fit it evenly.

18. Pierce the dough's bottom with a fork and let it chill in the refrigerator for 30 minutes.

19. Separate the egg and put the yolk in a small bowl. Reserve the white for the topping.

20. Mix the egg yolk with the chives, ½ cup of parmesan, 1 tablespoon olive oil, and the ricotta.

21. Remove the tart dough from the refrigerator and spread the egg yolk mixture across the tart shells' bottom.

22. Add the onions and scatter the mushrooms on top.

23. Beat the egg white in a small bowl with the remaining ¼ cup of parmesan and heavy cream.

24. Place the mixture over the mushrooms.

25. Cover the tart with foil and bake in the preheated oven for 30 minutes.

26. Remove the foil and bake for 15 minutes or until the crust turns light brown.

27. Garnish with microgreens and thyme and serve warm.

Huckleberry Cheesecake

Who can resist a delicious cheesecake? This recipe is easy to make and is the perfect dessert for you and your family.

Crust Ingredients:

- ½ cup of melted butter
- 1 (14.4 ounces) package of crushed graham crackers

Filling Ingredients:

- 1 cup of white sugar
- 1 (12-ounce) container of frozen, thawed whipped topping
- 2 (8-ounce) packages of softened cream cheese

Topping Ingredients:

- 1 cup of huckleberries
- ¼ cup of mashed huckleberries
- 1 teaspoon of lemon juice
- 1 pinch of salt
- 2 tablespoons of cornstarch
- ¾ cup of water
- 1 cup of white sugar
- 1 teaspoon of red food coloring (Optional)

Instructions:

1. Put the butter and graham cracker crumbs in a large bowl and mix until the crumbs are moistened.
2. Place over the bottom of a 9x13-inch baking pan and press to make the crust.
3. Put the 1 cup of sugar, whipped topping, and cream cheese in another bowl and mix until they turn smooth.
4. Spread over the crust.
5. Place the salt, cornstarch, water, and 1 cup of sugar in a saucepan and cook over medium heat for five minutes. Stir frequently.
6. Add the lemon juice, mashed huckleberries, and red food coloring (optional) to the cornstarch mixture and simmer for five minutes or until they thicken. Stir frequently.
7. Place the huckleberry mixture over the cream cheese.
8. Scatter whole huckleberries on top.
9. Let it chill before serving.

Dandelion Salad

Enjoy this tasty spring salad as a light breakfast, snack, or side dish.[66]

Enjoy this tasty spring salad as a light breakfast, snack, or side dish. The dandelion greens add a special taste to this healthy salad.

Ingredients:

- ½ pound of washed and torn dandelion greens
- ½ teaspoon of dried basil
- 2 chopped tomatoes
- ½ chopped red onion
- Salt and pepper to taste

Instructions:

1. Combine the tomatoes, red onion, and dandelion greens in a bowl.
2. Season with salt, pepper, and basil, and serve.

Sausage and Beef Stuffed Acorn Squash

This hearty meal is delicious and filling, making it the perfect lunch dish. The onions, sausage, beef, and acorns make this recipe irresistible.

Squash Ingredients:

- 1 seeded acorn squash, cut in halves
- Cooking spray
- Salt and pepper for seasoning

Filling Ingredients:

- 2 ounces of cubed cheddar cheese
- 1 minced clove garlic
- 1 small, chopped onion
- ¼ pound of ground pork sausage
- ¼ pound of lean ground beef
- 1 tablespoon of vegetable oil

Instructions:

1. Preheat the oven to 350° F.
2. Prepare the acorn squash by seasoning its flesh with salt and pepper.
3. Light coat the squash with cooking spray.
4. Put the squash cut sides down in a microwave-safe dish.
5. Cover with plastic wrap.
6. Microwave for 15 minutes or until the flesh is tender.
7. While the squash is microwaving, prepare the filling.
8. Put the oil in a skillet and heat over medium-high heat.
9. Add the sausage and beef and cook for nine minutes or until they turn crumbly and brown. Stir frequently.
10. Drain the grease from the skillet, but don't discard it. Put the meat in a bowl.
11. Cook the garlic and onion in a skillet with the grease for five minutes or until the onion turns translucent.
12. Remove from the heat.

13. Add the garlic mixture to the meat and sausage mixture, then add the cheddar cheese.
14. Put the acorn squash halves with the sides up on a baking sheet and add the filling with a spoon.
15. Bake uncovered in the oven for 20 minutes or until the squash turns light brown and the cheese melts.
16. Remove from the oven and season with salt and pepper to taste.
17. Serve hot.

Fireweed Jelly

Enjoy this homemade jelly with a tasty fireweed flavor on toast for a sugary and light breakfast.[66]

Enjoy this homemade jelly with a tasty fireweed flavor on toast for a sugary and light breakfast.

Ingredients:

- 10 cups of fireweed flowers
- 8 cups of sugar
- ¼ cup of lemon juice
- 4 packages of 1.75 ounces of powder pectin
- 8 cups of water

Instructions:

1. Put the blossoms in a large saucepan and fill it with water.
2. Boil for five minutes or until the water turns to a tea-like color.
3. Strain the liquid with a cheesecloth and place the liquid in a large stock pot.
4. Add the lemon juice and pectin and boil for one minute.
5. Add the sugar and boil for another minute. Stir frequently.
6. Sterilize the jars in which you will store the jam.
7. While the jars are hot, fill them with jelly using a ladle. Leave half-inch headspace.
8. Seal the jars tightly.
9. Process in hot water for 15 minutes.
10. Let the jars cool down on a hard surface for 24 hours.

Porcini Mushroom Lasagna

The porcini mushrooms give the lasagna a strong flavor. This dish is creamy, filling, and delicious.

Ingredients:

- 1 box of no-boil lasagna noodles
- 2 cups of dried porcini mushrooms
- 6 peeled and diced shallots
- 6 tablespoons of all-purpose flour
- 1 pound of sliced baby bella mushrooms
- 1 stick of unsalted butter
- 1 cup of chicken broth
- 1 ball of shredded smoked mozzarella

- 4 cloves of minced garlic
- 2 teaspoons of fresh thyme
- 1 cup of shredded gruyere
- Freshly ground nutmeg
- 1 cup of white wine
- 2 tablespoons of extra virgin olive oil
- 1 cup of shredded fontina
- 1 cup of grated parmesan cheese
- ¼ cup of minced flat-leaf Italian parsley
- 3 cups of milk heated with 1 bay leaf
- Salt and fresh ground pepper
- 2 tablespoons of truffle oil (optional)

Instructions:

1. Preheat the oven to 375 ° F.
2. Put 2 cups of hot chicken stock in a large saucepan.
3. Soak the mushrooms until they are softened.
4. Chop up the mushrooms and let them drain.
5. Prepare the bechamel sauce by melting the butter in a medium saucepan over medium heat.
6. Add the flour and let it cook for three minutes while whisking.
7. Add the heated milk but remove the bay leaf and whisk until it turns smooth.
8. Simmer for ten minutes or until the mixture is thickened.
9. Season with the nutmeg, salt, and pepper.
10. Reserve 1 ½ cups of sauce.
11. Prepare the mushrooms by adding two tablespoons of olive oil in a large sauté pan.
12. Add the shallots and garlic, and sauté for two minutes or until they soften.
13. Add the mushrooms and cook until they are done.
14. Add the thyme and parsley and deglaze the pan with the white wine.

15. Season with salt and pepper.
16. Add the porcinis and mushrooms to the large portion of béchamel and stir.
17. Add the ¼ cup of fontina, mozzarella, and gruyere and stir.
18. Add the truffle oil (optional).
19. Pour one cup of béchamel on the pan's bottom.
20. Add a layer of pasta.
21. Add some mushrooms and béchamel sauce.
22. Add a little of each cheese.
23. Add another layer of pasta and repeat the previous two steps.
24. Repeat until you run out of mushrooms.
25. Add pasta for the last layer and cover with the remaining béchamel.
26. Sprinkle parmesan cheese on top.
27. Bake in the preheated oven for 45 minutes or until the top turns golden brown.

Blackberry Puff Pastry Tarts

This dessert is for everyone with a sweet tooth."

This dessert is for everyone with a sweet tooth. You can serve it warm or cool. However, don't refrigerate or heat it in the microwave.

Ingredients:

- 1 ½ cups of frozen or fresh blackberries
- ¼ cup of turbinado sugar
- ¼ cup of milk
- ½ teaspoon of ground cinnamon
- ½ cup of white sugar
- 1 (8 ounces) package of room-temperature cream cheese
- 1 (10-ounce) package of frozen-thawed puff pastry shells

Instructions:

1. Preheat the oven to 375 ° F.
2. Grease a cookie sheet with cooking spray.
3. Put the cinnamon, sugar, and cream cheese in a bowl. Mix until they are blended, and set it aside.
4. Put the puff pastry shells on the cookie sheet.
5. Brush each shell with milk and sprinkle the sugar.
6. Bake the pastry shells in the oven for 15 minutes or until they turn golden brown and expand.
7. Don't overbake the shells, but ensure they are thoroughly baked.
8. Remove the cookie sheet from the oven and remove the cap from each shell with a fork. Put the caps aside.
9. Put two tablespoons of the cream cheese mixture in each shell.
10. Place six to eight blackberries on top.
11. Replace the caps to cover the berries.
12. Place the cookie sheet in the oven again and bake for five minutes or until the filling is warm and the caps turn golden brown.

Chanterelle Pizza

Don't waste your money on takeaway pizza. Make your own at home with this simple, tasty recipe.

Ingredients:

- 1 pizza dough ball
- 1 lemon
- 1 ½ ounces of mild brie, cut into small cubes
- 4 ounces of mozzarella, cut into cubes
- ½ cup of extra virgin olive oil
- 1 garlic clove
- 3 large handfuls of arugula
- 1 tablespoon of unsalted butter
- 1 cup of clean and trimmed chanterelles
- 2 green onions
- Salt and pepper to taste

Instructions:

1. Preheat the oven to 550°F and place the pizza stone inside.
2. Slice the two green onions and remove the upper green leafy part.
3. Put one tablespoon of butter in a wide pan and melt on medium heat.
4. Add one cup of trimmed chanterelles, green onions, and salt and pepper to taste.
5. Cook over high heat for two minutes or until tender and stir.
6. Blend most of the arugula, ½ teaspoon of salt, ½ cup of olive oil, and the garlic clove in a blender.
7. Add more olive oil if necessary to make it more drizzleable.
8. Stretch the pizza dough to a 12-inch circle and brush with olive oil.
9. Add three ounces of mozzarella cubes over the pizza dough, then add one and a half ounces of brie.
10. Place the pizza on the preheated stone and bake until the cheese melts and the pizza crust turns golden brown.
11. Drizzle the arugula sauce over the cooked pizza base, add the lemon zest, and serve.

Lobster Mushroom Pasta

This simple recipe is perfect for vegetarians looking for a meat-free and highly nutritious pasta dish.⁴⁸

This simple recipe is perfect for vegetarians looking for a meat-free and highly nutritious pasta dish.

Ingredients:

- 1 cup of fresh, clean, and sliced lobster mushrooms
- 8 ounces of dry fettuccine pasta
- ½ cup of heavy cream
- ½ cup of shredded parmesan cheese
- 2 tablespoons of olive oil
- 4 tablespoons of salted butter
- 3 minced clove garlic
- ½ teaspoon of ground black pepper (optional)
- 2 teaspoons of chopped parsley for garnish

Instructions:

1. Prepare the lobster mushrooms by washing them thoroughly.
2. Cut the mushrooms into thin slices.
3. Fill a large pot of water and boil on medium heat.

4. Add the pasta and cook for 12 minutes or until the pasta is tender.

5. Put the olive oil and butter in a sauté pan and heat over medium-high heat.

6. Add the mushrooms to the pan and cook for four minutes or until they are cooked and soft.

7. Add the garlic and black pepper (optional) and cook for 30 seconds.

8. Add the shredded parmesan cheese and heavy cream to the mushrooms and cook for two minutes or until the sauce thickens.

9. Add the cooked pasta and stir to mix.

10. Place on a big plate, garnish with chopped parsley and serve.

Pine Nut and Date Smoothie

Refresh yourself in the morning with this cool and healthy smoothie.

Ingredients:

- ¾ cup of pine nuts
- 1 ¼ cups of chopped pitted dates
- 3 cups of whole milk
- 1 tablespoon of honey
- 1 ½ cups of crushed ice

Instructions:

1. Put the pine nuts, dates, and milk in a blender and cover it. Don't blend.

2. Let them chill in the blender for 20 minutes.

3. Next, add the crushed ice and honey and blend until smooth.

4. Pour into two glasses and serve.

Watercress, Avocado, and Lime Smoothie

This smoothie is healthy, tasty, and refreshing.[69]

This smoothie has everything you are looking for and more. It is healthy, tasty, and refreshing.

Ingredients:

- 1 bag of watercress
- 1 small, peeled avocado with the seed removed
- 1 cup of chilled coconut water
- Small handful of mint leaves
- 1 peeled lime
- 1 ounce of baby spinach
- 1 and a half ounces of diced fresh or frozen pineapple

Instructions:

1. Blend all the ingredients in a blender until they are smooth.
2. Add more coconut water if you want a smoother consistency.
3. Keep in the fridge for up to three days or serve immediately.

Blackberry Frozen Yogurt

Enjoy this healthy snack to cool yourself during the summer.

Ingredients:

- 1 and a half cups of fresh blackberries
- 4 cups of plain Greek yogurt
- 1 cup of honey
- One drop or two of pure vanilla extract (optional)

Instructions:

1. Process the blackberries in a food processor until they turn smooth.
2. Strain the blackberries with a sieve over a large mixing bowl.
3. Press over the sieve with a spoon to squeeze out the juice.
4. Discard the pulp and seeds.
5. Add the yogurt and stir to mix.
6. Add ¾ cup of honey and taste. (Add more honey if you prefer).
7. Add the vanilla (optional) and mix to combine.
8. Process in an ice cream maker for 30 minutes or according to the manufacturer's instructions.
9. Serve soft or leave in the freezer for four hours.

Enjoy these delicious recipes and surprise your family or friends with a new and unique dish every day. Get creative and experiment with different ingredients if you are an experienced cook.

Chapter 7: Medicinal Plants of the Pacific Northwest

Using plants for healing is called herbal medicine, which dates back to ancient civilizations and has been a cornerstone of human healthcare for thousands of years.[70]

Using plants for healing is called herbal medicine, which dates back to ancient civilizations and has been a cornerstone of human healthcare for thousands of years. Ancient Egyptians, Chinese, Greeks, and Indians, among others, relied on the therapeutic qualities of plants to treat various ailments. Historical records, like the Ebers Papyrus from Egypt (circa 1550 BCE), document the extensive use of herbs like garlic and juniper for their medicinal benefits. Similarly, Traditional Chinese Medicine (TCM), with texts like the Shennong Ben Cao Jing from around 200 BCE, outlines numerous herbal uses for promoting health and treating diseases.

The Father of Medicine, Hippocrates, advocated for herbal remedies in ancient Greece. His work laid the foundation for later herbal traditions, including the Romans and medieval European herbalists. In India, one of the world's oldest holistic healing systems, Ayurveda has utilized plants like turmeric and ashwagandha for over 3,000 years.

The transition of plant-based medicine into modern times highlights its effectiveness. There is a growing emphasis on natural and integrative approaches to well-being in holistic health practices. Modern herbal medicine combines traditional knowledge with scientific research, validating the therapeutic properties of plants and incorporating them into complementary and alternative medicine (CAM).

For example, Echinacea boosts the immune system, ginger alleviates nausea, and valerian root promotes sleep. These are examples of how ancient herbal wisdom is applied today. The increased interest in plant-based remedies nowadays shows a broader trend toward seeking natural, sustainable, and holistic healthcare methods.

The tradition of using plants for healing is a long and enduring relationship between humans and nature. Its roots in ancient cultures show the timeless value of botanical remedies. At the same time, its relevance in modern holistic health practices highlights a continued commitment to natural wellness and integrating ancient wisdom with scientific understanding.

Medicinal Plant Profiles

You can forage amazing and extremely beneficial medicinal plants in the Pacific Northwest, such as:

Oregon Grape (*Mahonia aquifolium*)

Oregon Grape is a perennial evergreen shrub native to the Pacific Northwest.[71]

Oregon Grape is a perennial evergreen shrub native to the Pacific Northwest. It has glossy, holly-like leaves, bright yellow flowers, and deep purple berries. Oregon Grape often grows in forests and along stream banks, thriving in shaded, moist environments.

Traditional Uses

Indigenous tribes used the roots and bark of Oregon Grapes for their antibacterial and anti-inflammatory properties. The plant was commonly used to treat skin conditions, digestive issues, and infections. It was also employed in traditional ceremonies and as a yellow dye.

Therapeutic Properties

Oregon Grape contains berberine, a potent antimicrobial compound that is effective against various bacteria, fungi, and protozoa and is beneficial for treating infections. Its anti-inflammatory properties help reduce inflammation, making it useful for conditions like arthritis and various skin disorders like psoriasis and eczema. Moreover, it acts as a digestive aid by stimulating liver function and bile production, aiding digestion and detoxification. It is often used to treat issues like indigestion and liver congestion.

Stinging Nettle *(Urtica dioica)*

Stinging Nettle is an herbaceous perennial known for its stinging hairs, which cause mild irritation when touched. It grows in forests, meadows, and riverbanks, featuring serrated leaves and small, greenish flowers.

Traditional Uses

Stinging nettle has traditionally been used as a nutritive tonic to alleviate joint pain and allergies. Indigenous peoples used it for its fiber and as a food source after careful preparation to neutralize its sting.

Therapeutic Properties

Stinging Nettle is highly valued for its anti-inflammatory properties, which help reduce inflammation and pain, particularly in conditions like arthritis and other inflammatory joint diseases. Rich in vitamins A, C, and K and minerals like iron, calcium, and magnesium, it is a potent nutritive tonic supporting overall health and well-being. Its antihistamine effects effectively relieve hay fever symptoms and other allergic reactions, while its diuretic properties help manage urinary issues and support kidney function.

Red Clover *(Trifolium pratense)*

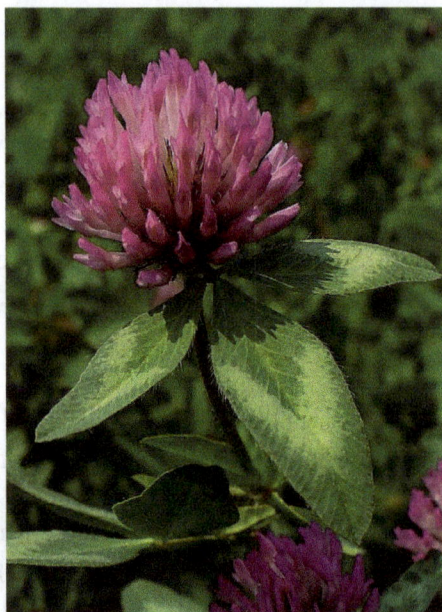

Red Clover is a short-lived perennial with distinctive pinkish-red flowers and trifoliate leaves.[73]

Red Clover is a short-lived perennial with distinctive pinkish-red flowers and trifoliate leaves. It thrives in well-drained, fertile soil and is commonly found in meadows, along roadsides, and pastures.

Traditional Uses

Indigenous people and later herbalists used red clover for its blood-purifying and anti-inflammatory properties. It was also used to treat coughs and skin conditions and as a general tonic.

Therapeutic Properties

Red Clover acts as a blood purifier, helping to remove toxins from the body and supporting overall detoxification processes. Its anti-inflammatory properties reduce inflammation and help with skin conditions like eczema and psoriasis. Containing phytoestrogens, Red Clover provides hormonal support instrumental in alleviating menopausal symptoms like hot flashes and mood swings. Furthermore, it supports cardiovascular health by improving circulation and reducing cholesterol levels.

Devil's Club (*Oplopanax horridus*)

Devil's Club is a large, spiny shrub found in the damp, forested regions of the Pacific Northwest. It features large, maple-like leaves, small white flowers, and clusters of bright red berries with spiny stems.

Traditional Uses

A sacred plant for many Indigenous tribes, Devil's Club was used for a wide range of ailments, including respiratory and digestive issues and spiritual protection. It was also used in ceremonial practices and as a general tonic to strengthen the body.

Therapeutic Properties

Devil's Club is recognized as an adaptogen. It helps the body adapt to stress and supports adrenal gland function, which is crucial for managing chronic stress and fatigue. Its anti-inflammatory properties effectively treat arthritis and other inflammatory conditions, relieving pain and swelling. Its antimicrobial effects help treat infections and support the immune system. Traditionally, it has been used to regulate blood sugar and as a remedy for colds and flu.

Yarrow (*Achillea millefolium*)

Yarrow is a hardy perennial with feathery leaves and small, white, or sometimes pink flower clusters.[78]

Yarrow is a hardy perennial with feathery leaves and small, white, or sometimes pink flower clusters. It thrives in various habitats, including meadows, coastal areas, and forest edges.

Traditional Uses

Indigenous people widely used yarrow for wound healing and fever reduction. It was employed in traditional rituals and as a remedy for digestive and menstrual problems.

Therapeutic Properties

Yarrow is highly regarded for its astringent properties, which help stop bleeding and promote wound healing, making it a valuable herb for treating cuts, abrasions, and other minor injuries. Its anti-inflammatory effects reduce inflammation, which is beneficial for treating wounds, skin conditions, and digestive tract inflammation. Yarrow possesses antipyretic properties, helping reduce fever and alleviate symptoms of colds and flu by promoting sweating. Furthermore, it can help with menstrual issues by regulating the menstrual cycle and alleviating cramps.

Licorice Root (*Glycyrrhiza spp.*)

Licorice is a perennial herb with long, wrinkled roots that have a sweet taste. It is found in various regions, including the Pacific Northwest, typically in well-drained soils and sunny locations.

Traditional Uses

Licorice root has been used in traditional medicine systems like Traditional Chinese Medicine (TCM) and Ayurveda for its soothing properties and for treating respiratory and digestive issues. It was used as a flavoring agent and in various traditional confections.

Therapeutic Properties

Licorice root is valued for its anti-inflammatory properties, which help reduce inflammation, particularly in the digestive tract. It is beneficial for conditions like gastritis and peptic ulcers. As an expectorant, it aids in clearing mucus from the respiratory tract, relieving coughs and bronchial conditions. Licorice root supports adrenal gland function, helping the body cope with stress and improving energy. It has been used for its antiviral and antimicrobial properties, helpful in treating infections and boosting the immune system

Echinacea (*Echinacea spp.*)

Echinacea, or coneflower, is a perennial herb with purple, daisy-like flowers and a prominent central cone.[74]

Echinacea, or coneflower, is a perennial herb with purple, daisy-like flowers and a prominent central cone. It is typically found in prairies, open woods, and gardens, thriving in well-drained soils.

Traditional Uses

Echinacea was a staple in traditional medicine for its immune-boosting properties. Native American tribes used it to treat infections, wounds, and snake bites.

Therapeutic Properties

Echinacea is renowned for its immune support, helping to boost the immune system and prevent colds, flu, and other infections. Its antimicrobial properties effectively fight against various bacteria and viruses, aiding in treating respiratory diseases and skin wounds. Furthermore, Echinacea has anti-inflammatory effects, reducing inflammation, supporting wound healing, and alleviating symptoms of chronic inflammatory conditions. Moreover, it enhances lymphatic function, promoting detoxification and overall immune health.

Black Cohosh (*Actaea racemosa*)

Black Cohosh is a tall, flowering plant with white, feathery blooms and large, compound leaves. It is native to the woodlands of North America and prefers shaded, moist environments.

Traditional Uses

Indigenous tribes and early settlers used it for women's health issues, particularly menopausal symptoms and menstrual discomfort. It was also used for its sedative properties and to treat rheumatic pain.

Therapeutic Properties

Black Cohosh provides hormonal support, helping to alleviate menopausal symptoms like hot flashes, night sweats, and mood swings by mimicking estrogen's effects on the body. Its anti-inflammatory properties reduce inflammation and pain, which is particularly useful in treating arthritis and muscle pain. As a nervine, Black Cohosh calms the nervous system, helping to relieve anxiety, irritability, and sleep disturbances associated with menopause and premenstrual syndrome. Also, it is used to support uterine health and regulate menstrual cycles.

Cascara Sagrada *(Rhamnus purshiana)*

Clusters of yellow flowers bloom in the spring, followed by dark purple berries that mature in the fall.[75]

Cascara sagrada is a small tree native to the Pacific Northwest forests. It can grow up to 30 feet tall and has smooth, greyish bark that becomes rough with age. Clusters of yellow flowers bloom in the spring, followed by dark purple berries that mature in the fall.

Traditional Uses

Indigenous tribes in the Pacific Northwest used cascara sagrada as a laxative to treat constipation. The bark was harvested, dried, and steeped in water to make tea.

The essential medicinal components of cascara sagrada are cascarosides, specifically cascarosides A, B, C, and D. These compounds act as stimulant laxatives by increasing fluid secretion in the colon and stimulating muscle contractions.

Therapeutic Properties

Cascara sagrada is an effective laxative. However, its use should be limited due to potential side effects like abdominal cramping, dehydration, and electrolyte imbalance. Long-term use can lead to dependence and weaken colon muscles.

Cascara sagrada is not recommended for children, pregnant or breastfeeding women, or people with medical conditions like intestinal blockage or inflammatory bowel disease. It can interact with other medications, so consult a healthcare professional before use.

Epazote *(Dysphania ambrosioides)*

Epazote is a leafy green herb native to Central and South America but has adapted well to the Pacific Northwest climate. It has a strong, pungent odor due to the essential oils present. The leaves are lance-shaped with serrated edges and grow on a branching stem that can reach up to 5 feet tall.

Traditional Uses

Traditionally, epazote has been used as a natural dewormer to expel intestinal parasites, particularly roundworms. The plant's aerial parts, including the leaves and stems, were used to make a tea or tincture.

Therapeutic Properties

Epazote is effective against some intestinal worms. However, ascaridole is toxic to humans in high doses and can cause nausea, vomiting, seizures, and even death when used in copious amounts.

Peppermint *(Mentha piperita)*

Peppermint is a fragrant, herbaceous perennial known for its refreshing aroma and taste.[76]

Peppermint is a fragrant, herbaceous perennial known for its refreshing aroma and taste. It thrives in moist environments throughout the Pacific Northwest. Square stems have clusters of small purple flowers and dark green leaves with serrated edges.

Traditional Uses

Peppermint has been a popular remedy for indigenous people to relieve nausea, indigestion, and heartburn. They would often chew on the leaves or steep them in hot water to make tea.

Therapeutic Properties

Peppermint can relieve nausea, stop vomiting, soothe indigestion, reduce heartburn, relax muscle spasms in the digestive tract, and promote bile flow.

Peppermint is a widely used OTC treatment for various digestive ailments. It is available in various forms, including teas, capsules, tinctures, and essential oils. Peppermint oil can also be applied topically to relieve muscle aches and headaches.

General Disclaimer

The information about medicinal plants is for educational purposes only and is not intended as medical advice. Always consult a qualified healthcare provider before using any plant for medicinal purposes. Never self-diagnose or self-medicate, as improper use of herbal remedies can lead to adverse effects and interactions with other medications or underlying health conditions. Your healthcare provider can help determine the appropriate treatment for your specific health needs and ensure that herbal remedies are safe and effective.

Methods for Preparation

Teas and Infusions

Herbal Teas: To make a basic herbal tea, steep 1-2 teaspoons of dried herbs (or 2-3 teaspoons of fresh herbs) in a cup of boiling water for 5-10 minutes. Strain and enjoy.

Infusions: For a more robust preparation, infuse herbs in hot water for an extended period. Place 1-2 tablespoons of dried herbs in a jar, pour boiling water over them, cover, and let steep for 4-8 hours. Strain before drinking.

Examples

Chamomile Tea: Known for its calming properties, it promotes sleep and reduces anxiety.

Peppermint Tea: Helps soothe digestive issues and relieve headaches.

Tinctures

Tinctures are concentrated herbal extracts processed by soaking herbs in alcohol or vinegar. Fill a jar halfway with dried herbs, then fill the jar to the top with alcohol (like vodka) or vinegar. Seal the jar and let it sit in a cool, dark place for 4-6 weeks, shaking it occasionally. Strain the liquid into a dropper bottle.

Administration

Take tinctures in small doses, usually 1-2 dropperfuls (about 20-40 drops) diluted in water or juice, 2-3 times a day.

Examples

Echinacea Tincture: Boosts the immune system and helps fight colds and infections.

Valerian Root Tincture: It can be used as a sedative to help you sleep and reduce anxiety.

Poultices and Compresses

Poultices: Crush fresh herbs or mix dried herbs with hot water to form a paste. Apply the paste directly to the skin, cover it with a cloth, and leave it on for 20-30 minutes.

Compresses: Soak a cloth in a robust herbal tea or infusion and apply it to the affected area.

Examples

Comfrey Poultice: Used to reduce inflammation and promote the healing of bruises, sprains, and broken bones.

Chamomile Compress: Helps soothe irritated skin and reduce inflammation.

Salves and Ointments

Combine herbal or infused oils with beeswax to make salves. Fill a jar with dried herbs and cover with olive oil to make an infused oil. Let it sit in a sunny spot for 2-4 weeks, then strain. Melt 1 ounce of beeswax in a double boiler, add 1 cup of the infused oil, and pour into containers to cool.

Examples

Calendula Salve: Used for its healing and anti-inflammatory properties, ideal for cuts, scrapes, and minor burns.

Arnica Salve: Helps reduce pain and inflammation from bruises and sprains.

Syrups

Herbal syrups combine strong herbal teas or decoctions with honey or sugar. Simmer herbs in water until the liquid is reduced by half. Strain, then add an equal amount of honey or sugar. Store in a refrigerator and use within a few months.

Examples

Elderberry Syrup: Popular for its immune-boosting properties, especially during the cold and flu season.

Ginger Syrup: Helps soothe sore throats and relieves nausea.

Capsules and Tablets

Dried herbs can be ground into a fine powder and encapsulated using empty capsules available from health stores. This method is helpful for herbs that may have an unpleasant taste.

Examples

Turmeric Capsules: Taken for their anti-inflammatory and antioxidant benefits.

Milk Thistle Capsules: Supports liver health and detoxification.

Practical Tips for Everyday Use

- Introduce one herb at a time to monitor its effects on your body.
- Use high-quality, organic herbs to ensure the best therapeutic benefits.
- Regularly using medicinal herbs can offer cumulative benefits, so incorporate them into your daily routine.
- Always label your preparations with the herb's name and the preparation date. Store them in a cool, dark place to maintain their potency.

- Add dried or fresh herbs to your bathwater for a relaxing and therapeutic soak.
- Integrate medicinal herbs like basil, oregano, and turmeric into your cooking for added health benefits.
- Infuse vinegar or oil with herbs for use in salad dressings, marinades, or as a base for massage oils.
- Mix herbs with honey and let it infuse for natural sweetening and medicinal properties.
- Inhale steam from a bowl of hot water infused with herbs to relieve respiratory issues.
- Use herbal infusions as facial toners to benefit from their astringent and soothing properties.
- Add herbs to your water for hydration with added health benefits.
- Freeze herbs in ice cube trays for flavorful and medicinal additions to drinks or soups.
- Powders and Mouthwashes: Use herbal toothpowder and mouthwash for oral health.
- Infuse vinegar with antimicrobial herbs for natural cleaning solutions.
- Place herb-filled sachets in drawers or under pillows for calming and aromatic effects.
- Soak your feet in hot water with herbs to relax and treat minor foot issues.
- Fill capsules with powdered herbs for convenient ingestion of medicinal plants.

Disclaimer: Always consult a healthcare provider before incorporating medicinal plants into your routine, especially if you are pregnant, breastfeeding, or have a medical condition. Never self-diagnose or self-medicate.

Potential Risks Associated with Using Medicinal Plants

While medicinal plants offer numerous health benefits, it is crucial to approach their use with caution. Understanding safety considerations, potential risks, and proper dosage guidelines is essential to avoid adverse effects and ensure effective treatment.

Allergic Reactions

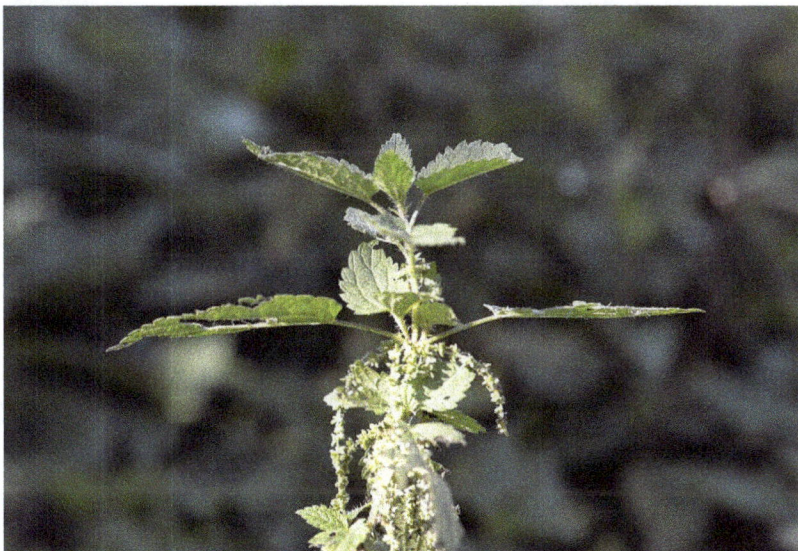

Some plants, like Stinging Nettle, can cause skin irritation upon contact.[77]

Some plants, like Stinging Nettle, can cause skin irritation upon contact. Always test a small area of skin before using a new herb topically. Inhaling certain herbs or their essential oils can trigger respiratory reactions in sensitive individuals.

Consuming herbal preparations can sometimes cause allergic reactions, including hives, itching, and gastrointestinal distress.

Guidelines

Conduct a patch test before applying a new herb or herbal preparation to a larger skin area. When ingesting a new herb, begin with a small dose to monitor for adverse reactions.

Interactions with Medications

Herbs like Ginkgo Biloba and Garlic can potentiate the effects of blood thinners, increasing the risk of bleeding. Some herbs, like Licorice

Root, can affect blood pressure, potentially interfering with blood pressure medications.

Like Ginseng, herbs affecting blood sugar levels can interact with diabetes medications, requiring dosage adjustments.

Guidelines

Always inform your healthcare provider about the herbal supplements you are taking, especially if you are on prescription medications. Monitor your condition closely if you use an herb that could potentially interact with your medications.

Dosage Guidelines

The potency of herbs can vary widely depending on their source, preparation method, and part of the plant used. People can react differently to the same herb, with some being more sensitive and others more tolerant. Prolonged use of certain herbs can lead to side effects or diminished effectiveness.

Guidelines

Adhere to dosage recommendations provided by qualified healthcare providers or detailed on product labels. Begin with the lowest recommended dose and gradually increase if necessary, observing for adverse effects. Take periodic breaks from certain herbs to avoid the potential buildup of active compounds in your system.

Specific Herb Risks

Oregon Grape *(Mahonia aquifolium)*

Risk: High doses can cause gastrointestinal upset.

Use under supervision if you have existing liver conditions or are taking other liver-affecting medications.

Stinging Nettle *(Urtica dioica)*

Risk: Can cause skin irritation and may interact with diuretics.

Wear gloves when handling and consult a healthcare provider if you have kidney issues.

Red Clover *(Trifolium pratense)*

Risk: Contains phytoestrogens that can interact with hormone therapy and anticoagulants.

Avoid if you have hormone-sensitive conditions or are on blood-thinning medications.

Devil's Club *(Oplopanax horridus)*

Risk: Potential hypoglycemic effects.

People with diabetes should use it cautiously and monitor blood sugar levels closely.

Yarrow *(Achillea millefolium)*

Risk: Can cause photosensitivity and allergic skin reactions.

Avoid prolonged sun exposure after topical use and do a patch test first.

Licorice Root *(Glycyrrhiza spp.)*

Risk: Long-term use can lead to high blood pressure and low potassium levels.

Limit use to short periods and avoid if you have hypertension or potassium deficiency.

Echinacea *(Echinacea spp.)*

Risk: It can cause allergic reactions in individuals sensitive to plants in the Daisy family.

Use cautiously if you have allergies to ragweed, marigolds, or daisies.

Black Cohosh *(Actaea racemosa)*

Risk: It may cause gastrointestinal upset and interact with hormone-sensitive treatments.

Avoid if you have a history of liver disease or breast cancer. Consult a healthcare provider before use.

General Safety Tips

- Ensure you source high-quality, organic herbs from reputable suppliers to avoid contaminants.

- Store herbs and herbal preparations in a cool, dry place to maintain potency and prevent spoilage.

- Please educate yourself about each herb you plan to use, including its benefits, potential side effects, and contraindications.

Disclaimer: Always consult a healthcare provider before using any medicinal plants, especially if you are pregnant, breastfeeding, have a medical condition, or are taking other medications. Never self-diagnose or self-medicate. Proper guidance ensures the safe and effective use of herbal remedies in your wellness routine.

Continued Learning in Herbalism

The world of herbalism is vast and continually evolving, showcasing centuries of accumulated knowledge and modern scientific discoveries. As with any field of natural medicine, ongoing learning and exploration are crucial for safely and effectively integrating medicinal plants into your health regimen. Here's why continued education and curiosity are essential in herbalism:

Evolving Knowledge

Herbalism is grounded in tradition but continually benefits from new research and discoveries.[78]

Herbalism is grounded in tradition but continually benefits from new research and discoveries. Scientists and herbalists constantly uncover new information about plant compounds, their interactions, and health benefits. Staying informed about the latest findings ensures you use herbs most effectively and safely.

Action Steps

- Subscribe to journals and publications focused on herbal medicine.
- Participate in events where experts share the latest developments and techniques.

Comprehensive Understanding

Medicinal plants can have complex effects on the body. Understanding each herb's properties, potential interactions, and contraindications is vital to using them safely and effectively. This comprehensive knowledge helps prevent adverse effects and maximizes the therapeutic benefits of herbal remedies.

Action Steps

- Learn about the historical and cultural contexts of different medicinal plants.
- Read various herbalists' books, articles, and guides to gain diverse perspectives.

Personal Experience

Each person's body is unique, and herbal remedies can affect individuals differently. Guided by thorough research and professional advice, personal experimentation allows you to discover what works best for your specific needs and conditions.

Action Steps

- Document your experiences with different herbs, noting dosages, effects, and side effects.
- Introduce new herbs gradually and monitor your body's responses.

Building a Community

Engaging with a community of fellow herbalists and enthusiasts can provide support, share experiences, and offer diverse insights. Collaborative learning enhances your knowledge and helps you stay motivated and inspired.

Action Steps

- Participate in local or online herbalism communities and forums.
- Teach others what you have learned and learn from their experiences.

Ethical Practices

Ongoing education includes understanding the environmental impact of harvesting medicinal plants. Learning about sustainable practices ensures you contribute to the conservation of plant species and their habitats.

Action Steps

- Follow guidelines to avoid overharvesting and ensure plant populations remain healthy.
- Purchase herbs from reputable sources that prioritize sustainability and fair trade.

Encouraging Curiosity

Continued curiosity and a passion for learning will enrich your journey in herbalism. Digging deeper into medicinal plants study enhances your ability to use them wisely and responsibly.

Action Steps

- Enroll in advanced herbalism courses and certifications.
- Expand your repertoire by learning about less common medicinal plants and their uses.

Herbalism offers endless opportunities for learning and personal growth. Committing to ongoing education enhances your health and well-being and enables you to develop a broader understanding of natural medicine. Keep exploring to retain the wisdom of medicinal plants, enriching your life in countless ways.

Disclaimer: Always consult a healthcare provider before using any medicinal plants, especially if you are pregnant, breastfeeding, have a medical condition, or are taking other medications. Never self-diagnose or self-medicate. Proper guidance ensures the safe and effective use of herbal remedies in your wellness routine.

Chapter 8: Is a Foraging Lifestyle for You?

So, how do you know if a foraging lifestyle is what you want? Can you go from modern living to a foraging lifestyle? It's not as simple as waking up one day and deciding to eat the berries you find in the woods. Making this transition is a journey that requires a shift in mindset and daily habits. However, it's a rewarding adventure that brings you closer to nature, offers a more sustainable way of living, and opens up a world of culinary delights.

Have you ever wanted to step outside and gather your breakfast from your backyard or a nearby forest? Imagine waking up on a crisp autumn morning, putting on your boots, and heading out to collect wild mushrooms or fresh herbs. You might bring back a basket brimming with chanterelles, which you'll sauté with eggs for a delicious, earthy breakfast. Or maybe you'll find wild mint to add to your morning tea, infusing your day with the refreshing taste of nature.

Modern life can be fast-paced and overwhelming, with constant notifications and endless to-do lists."

Have you ever felt the need to slow down and reconnect with the world around you? Modern life can be fast-paced and overwhelming, with constant notifications and endless to-do lists. A foraging lifestyle encourages you to take a step back, breathe, and observe the subtle changes in the environment. You'll notice the first signs of spring in the budding leaves or how certain plants thrive after the rain. This mindfulness reduces stress and fosters a deeper appreciation for the natural world.

Do you sometimes crave a more sustainable way of living? Foraging helps reduce your reliance on grocery stores and the global supply chain, which can be environmentally taxing and disconnected from local ecosystems. Picture yourself making a hearty stew with wild garlic, dandelion greens, and nettles you've foraged. Not only are you reducing your carbon footprint, but you're also consuming foods free from pesticides and packaging. Each meal becomes a small act of environmental stewardship.

Have you ever wondered what it would be like to truly understand and utilize the plants around you? A foraging lifestyle transforms the way you see the world. Those weeds in your yard might be a source of nutritious greens. That tree you pass by every day could provide edible nuts or fruit.

You become a detective, learning to identify different species and their uses. This knowledge empowers you and connects you to human survival and ingenuity history.

Do you want to break free from the monotony of store-bought foods and explore new flavors sometimes? Foraging introduces you to a diverse palette of tastes you won't find in any supermarket. Imagine the tangy zest of wood sorrel in your salad or the sweet and tart burst of wild blackberries in your dessert. Each season brings new ingredients to experiment with, making your culinary adventures as varied as the landscape.

Living a foraging lifestyle isn't only about the food. It's about building a lifestyle emphasizing sustainability, community, and a profound connection to nature. You might share your foraging experiences with friends and family, inviting them to join you on outings or to taste your latest creations. You'll find yourself participating in local foraging groups, where knowledge is shared and communal bonds are strengthened.

But being realistic is essential. This lifestyle requires time, effort, and a willingness to learn. You can't forage everything you need to live, especially not right away. There will be challenges, like learning to identify plants accurately, finding safe foraging spots, and understanding local regulations. There will be days when you come home empty-handed or make a meal that doesn't turn out quite right. However, these moments are part of the journey and offer valuable lessons.

Ultimately, deciding if a foraging lifestyle is for you comes down to whether you're willing to embrace these challenges and joys. It's about more than finding food. It's about finding a deeper purpose and fulfillment in your relationship with the Earth. So, is it a foraging lifestyle for you? It's a question only you can answer, but if you're drawn to the idea of living more sustainably, connecting deeply with nature, and discovering new and exciting flavors, then perhaps it's a journey worth considering.

Reflecting on the Journey

As you reflect on your foraging journey, you should recognize how far you've come and the depth of knowledge you've gained. Think back to when you first started this journey – perhaps the concept of foraging was entirely new to you. You may have felt overwhelmed by the sheer amount of information and the potential risks of misidentifying plants. But look at you now. You've acquired skills many people don't possess – and you've cultivated a deeper appreciation for the natural world.

Consider the basics of foraging you've mastered. Do you remember your first successful forage? Maybe it was something simple like identifying dandelions in your backyard. You learned to distinguish their bright yellow flowers and jagged leaves from other plants. You discovered these common "weeds" are not only edible but also packed with nutrients. You've grown in confidence, moving on to more complex foraging challenges from that small success.

Think about the seasonal changes you've learned to recognize. You now understand that each season brings its own bounty. In spring, you eagerly anticipate the first shoots of wild asparagus poking through the soil. Summer brings an abundance of berries – blackberries, huckleberries, and salmonberries – that you eagerly gather for fresh eating or preserving. Autumn is the time for mushrooms, and you've learned to identify chanterelles and morels, savoring their rich, earthy flavors. While seemingly barren, winter offers hardy greens and roots that sustain you through the colder months.

Reflect on the specific plants and fungi you've learned to identify and harvest. Do you recall the satisfaction of finding your first patch of stinging nettles and knowing how to handle and prepare them? Or the thrill of stumbling upon a hidden grove of wild garlic, its pungent aroma guiding you? Each discovery added a new dimension to your knowledge and a new ingredient to your kitchen.

Think about the culinary skills you've developed. Foraging isn't only about gathering food. It's about transforming those ingredients into delicious meals. You've experimented with recipes, learning to incorporate wild ingredients into your everyday cooking. Maybe you've made a nettle pesto that became a family favorite or a wild berry jam your friends couldn't get enough of. Each dish you prepare tells a story of your journey and connection to the land.

Reflect on how your perception of the environment has changed. You now see the natural world as a backdrop to your life *and as an integral part.* You notice the subtle signs of the changing seasons, the intricate relationships between plants and animals, and the impact of weather patterns. This heightened awareness has made you more mindful of your actions and their environmental consequences.

Consider the personal growth you've experienced. Foraging requires patience, attention to detail, and resilience. You've faced challenges – days when you returned home empty-handed, plants that didn't turn out to be what you thought, and the weather that didn't cooperate, but these experiences have taught you valuable lessons. You've learned to persevere, adapt, and appreciate the journey as much as the destination.

Reflect on the fulfillment and joy you've found. Foraging is more than a hobby – it's a way of life bringing immense satisfaction. The simple act of gathering food from the wild connects you to your ancestors and the natural world profoundly. It's a reminder of the abundance nature offers and the importance of living in harmony with it.

As you reflect on your journey, take pride in what you've achieved. You've learned how to forage and gained a deeper understanding of the world around you. This journey has transformed you, fostering a greater appreciation for nature and more sustainable living. Remember, this is only the beginning. There's always more to learn, discover, and enjoy in the foraging world.

Celebrating the Seasons

Living a foraging lifestyle in the Pacific Northwest can bring you so much joy in the natural cycles and help you develop a keen awareness of the ever-changing landscape.[80]

Living a foraging lifestyle in the Pacific Northwest can bring you so much joy in the natural cycles and help you develop a keen awareness of the ever-changing landscape. With its diverse ecosystems ranging from coastal shores to lush forests and alpine meadows, the Pacific Northwest offers an incredible variety of wild foods that change with the seasons.

Spring is a time of renewal and awakening in the Pacific Northwest. As the days grow longer and the temperatures rise, the first signs of life emerge from the forest floor. Imagine the excitement of spotting the bright green shoots of stinging nettles pushing through the soil. These early greens are filled with nutrients and can make a nourishing nettle soup or a vibrant pesto. You've learned to handle them carefully to avoid their sting and appreciate their unique, slightly earthy flavor.

Spring also brings the delicate fiddlehead ferns, their tightly coiled fronds appearing like little green sculptures. You know you should harvest them while they are still young and tender before they unfurl into full-grown ferns. Lightly sautéed with garlic and lemon, fiddleheads add a crisp, fresh flavor to your meals.

Summer in the Pacific Northwest is a time of abundance. The forests and meadows burst with life, offering many wild berries. Picture yourself on a sunny afternoon, wandering through a berry patch, your fingers stained with the juice of ripe blackberries. You've learned to distinguish between the various berries – salmonberries with their unique orange hue, tart red huckleberries, and sweet, plump thimbleberries. Each has its distinct flavor and culinary uses. You gather them in baskets, envisioning homemade jams, pies, and berry-infused beverages.

In the heat of summer, you might forage along the coast. The Pacific Northwest is known for its coastal edibles, such as sea asparagus and beach greens. Imagine the salty breeze as you explore tide pools and rocky shores, collecting seaweed to dry for future use. Seaweed adds a savory umami flavor to soups and salads, and its nutritional benefits are unparalleled. These coastal foraging trips provide food and offer a refreshing escape from the inland heat.

As summer fades into fall, the forests take on a new character. Autumn is mushroom season in the Pacific Northwest, and the damp, cool weather creates perfect conditions for fungi to flourish. You've learned to identify the prized chanterelles hidden beneath the fallen leaves with their golden caps and fruity aroma. There's an adventure in hunting for mushrooms. It's a mix of patience and keen observation. You might find boletes, lobster mushrooms, and the highly sought-after matsutake, each adding unique flavors to your culinary repertoire.

Fall also brings a bounty of nuts and seeds. You've discovered the joy of foraging hazelnuts from the wild hazel trees growing abundantly in Oregon's Willamette Valley. Cracking their hard shells open to reveal the creamy nuts inside is satisfying. You can use them to make rich nut butter or enjoy them roasted. Once properly leached to remove their bitterness, acorns from oak trees can be ground into flour for baking. These autumn harvests connect you to the forest's cycles and provide sustenance as the days grow shorter.

Winter in the Pacific Northwest may seem like a time of scarcity, but there are still treasures to be found. Root vegetables, such as wild carrots and burdock, can be dug from the ground, adding hearty to your winter meals. You've learned to forage for miner's lettuce, a hardy green that thrives in the cooler months, adding fresh, peppery notes to your salads. Winter foraging teaches you resilience and resourcefulness as you find nourishment even on colder, darker days.

Living in tune with the seasons means understanding and respecting the natural cycles. You've developed the skills to recognize when plants and fungi are at their peak and when they must be left alone to regenerate. This sustainable approach ensures the bounty of the Pacific Northwest can be enjoyed for generations.

Celebrating the seasons through foraging deepens your connection to nature and enhances your appreciation for the natural world. Each season has challenges and rewards, teaching you to adapt and find joy in the changing landscape. The Pacific Northwest, with its rich and diverse ecosystems, offers endless opportunities to explore and discover.

Broader Implications of Foraging

Adopting a foraging lifestyle has profound implications extending beyond gathering wild foods. It positively impacts your personal health, contributes to environmental conservation, and fosters community engagement. Each aspect enriches your life, making foraging a holistic and sustainable way of living.

Foraging encourages you to eat a diverse range of fresh, nutrient-dense foods. Imagine incorporating wild greens like dandelion leaves and chickweed into your salads. These plants are abundant and packed with vitamins and minerals you might not get from typical grocery store produce. You've learned to forage for wild garlic, adding its pungent, flavorful bulbs to your cooking, boosting flavor and health benefits.

You improve your diet significantly by reducing reliance on processed foods. Consider replacing store-bought, sugary snacks with homemade energy bars made from foraged nuts and berries. You gather hazelnuts from local trees, roast them, and mix them with dried huckleberries and a bit of honey. These natural snacks are delicious and free from artificial additives and preservatives. Foraging empowers you to take control of your diet, making healthier choices that benefit your overall well-being.

Environmental conservation is another crucial aspect of foraging. Sourcing food locally and sustainably reduces your carbon footprint. Picture a typical day in the life of a forager: instead of driving to the supermarket, you walk or bike to nearby forests, meadows, and coastlines. This reduces fuel consumption and minimizes the environmental impact of food transportation and packaging. Each step you take in the forest leaves a lighter footprint than the industrial agriculture system.

Foraging teaches you to respect, appreciate, and protect natural habitats."

Moreover, foraging teaches you to respect and protect natural habitats. You've learned to harvest responsibly, only taking what you need and leaving enough for the plants and animals who rely on these resources. For example, when collecting mushrooms, you carefully cut the stems instead of pulling them out, ensuring the mycelium network remains intact. This practice supports the regeneration of mushroom populations and maintains the ecosystem's health.

Foraging promotes biodiversity. By appreciating and using a wide variety of wild plants, you help preserve species that might otherwise be overlooked or undervalued. Imagine the impact of choosing wildcrafted herbal teas made from nettles, elderflowers, and yarrows over commercial blends. Your choices support the conservation of these native species and encourage sustainable harvesting practices.

Furthermore, foraging can contribute to local food security. Tapping into the abundant natural resources around you reduces dependence on commercial food systems, which can be vulnerable to disruptions. Imagine a community where foraging is a common practice, and neighbors regularly share their wild harvests. This creates a resilient food network that is less susceptible to shortages and economic fluctuations.

On a larger scale, embracing a foraging lifestyle can influence broader cultural and societal shifts toward sustainability. Your choices and actions can inspire others to reconsider their relationship with food and the environment. There is a collective movement toward a more sustainable and mindful way of living as more people adopt foraging practices.

Continuing the Foraging Journey

As you continue your foraging journey beyond the pages of this book, you will encounter various opportunities for exploration and learning. Embrace these opportunities to deepen your connection with the natural world and expand your knowledge of wild foods.

Consider attending workshops and classes led by experienced foragers and herbalists. These hands-on learning experiences provide valuable insights into plant identification, ethical harvesting practices, and culinary uses of wild foods. Imagine participating in a wild mushroom foray led by a seasoned mycologist, learning to identify different species and distinguish between edible and poisonous mushrooms.

Joining a foraging group or club is another excellent way to expand your foraging horizons. Imagine being part of a community of foragers who organize regular outings, share tips and resources, and support each other in their foraging endeavors. You could participate in group hikes to explore new foraging spots, collaborate on community projects, like planting native edible gardens, or organize skill-sharing events where members teach each other about their favorite wild foods.

Spending more time in nature is perhaps the simplest yet most profound way to deepen your connection with the natural world. Imagine dedicating a few hours each week to exploring local parks, forests, and coastal areas, observing the seasonal changes, and discovering new foraging treasures. Take leisurely walks along woodland trails, pausing to examine the plants and fungi inhabiting the forest floor. Or venture to the shoreline, where the rhythm of the tides reveals hidden delicacies like seaweed and shellfish.

Consider incorporating foraging into your everyday life practically. Perhaps you could start a small herb garden in your backyard, where you grow culinary herbs, like mint, thyme, and oregano, alongside native medicinal plants like echinacea and lemon balm. These homegrown herbs provide a convenient and sustainable source of fresh flavors and healing remedies, complementing your foraging adventures in the wild. You could experiment with preserving seasonal harvests through techniques like drying, fermenting, and canning, ensuring a year-round supply of wild foods.

Embrace the spirit of creativity and experimentation in your foraging journey. You could invent new recipes combining wild ingredients' unique flavors and textures. You could create a wild greens pesto using a combination of foraged herbs like wild garlic, nettles, and sorrel, or concoct a wild berry chutney with a hint of wild ginger and spicebush. Let your imagination guide you as you explore the culinary possibilities of the natural world, adapting traditional recipes and techniques to incorporate wild ingredients in unexpected ways.

Ultimately, continuing your foraging journey is about embracing a lifelong commitment to learning, exploration, and stewardship. It's about deepening your connection with the natural world, fostering community connections, and sharing the Earth's abundance with others. As you embark on this next phase of your foraging adventure, approach it with curiosity, humility, and wonder. There is always more to discover, more to learn, and more to savor in the wild.

Bonus: Pacific Northwest Foraging Calendar

Pacific Northwest Foraging Calendar

❄ Winter ☘ Spring ☀ Summer 🍁 Fall	Jan	Feb	Mar	Apr	May	Jun	Jul	Aug	Sep	Oct	Nov	Dec
☘ SPRING												
Dandelion Greens			■	■	■	■						
Miner's Lettuce		■	■	■	■	■						
Wild Onions			■	■	■	■						
Wild Potatoes				■	■	■	■					
Wild Carrots				■	■	■	■					
Morels				■	■	■	■					
Stinging Nettle			■	■	■							
Red Columbine			■	■	■	■						
Elderflower				■	■	■						

	Jan	Feb	Mar	Apr	May	Jun	Jul	Aug	Sep	Oct	Nov	Dec

☀ **S U M M E R**

	Jan	Feb	Mar	Apr	May	Jun	Jul	Aug	Sep	Oct	Nov	Dec
Lamb's Quarters					■	■	■	■	☀			
Watercress					■	■	■	■	☀			
Fireweed					■	■	■	■	☀			
Wild Rose						■	■	☀				
Huckleberries							■	■	☀			
Salmonberries						■	■	■	☀			
Thimbleberries						■	■	■	☀			
Blackberries						■	■	■	☀			
Chanterelles						■	■	■	☀			
Lobster Mushrooms						■	■	■	☀			
Oyster Mushrooms					■	■	■	■	☀			
Lion's Mane								■	■	■	☀	
Porcini						■	■	■	■	■	☀	
Matsutake								■	■	■	☀	
Cauliflower Mushrooms							■	■	■	☀		
Chicken-of-the-Woods						■	■	■	☀			
Oregon Grape						■	■	■	■	☀		
Red Clover						■	■	☀				
Yarrow						■	■	■	☀			

	Jan	Feb	Mar	Apr	May	Jun	Jul	Aug	Sep	Oct	Nov	Dec
🍁 FALL												
Acorns									●	●	🍁	
Hazelnuts									●	●	🍁	
Pine Nuts									●	●	🍁	
Black Walnuts									●	●	🍁	
Camas									●	🍁		
Burdock								●	●	🍁		
Devil's Club									●	🍁		
Licorice Root									●	🍁		
Echinacea									●	🍁		
Black Cohosh									●	🍁		

	Jan	Feb	Mar	Apr	May	Jun	Jul	Aug	Sep	Oct	Nov	Dec
❄ WINTER												
Dandelion Greens	❄											❄
Watercress	❄											❄

Legend: ❄ Winter · 🍁 Spring · ☀ Summer · 🍁 Fall

Index: A-Z of Wild Edibles and Medicinal Plants

Toxic Plants and Fungi List

Death Camas *(Toxicoscordion venenosum)*

Looks Like: Wild Onion *(Allium spp.)*

Differentiating Factor: Death Camas has solid stems and lacks the onion/garlic smell when leaves are crushed, while Wild Onion has hollow stems and a distinct onion/garlic odor.

False Morel *(Gyromitra spp.)*

Looks Like: True Morel *(Morchella spp.)*

Differentiating Factor: False Morel has a brain-like or convoluted cap and can be reddish-brown to dark brown, while True Morel has a honeycomb-like cap with deep ridges and is usually yellow or gray.

Hemlock *(Conium maculatum)*

Looks Like: Queen Anne's Lace/Wild Carrot *(Daucus carota)*

Differentiating Factor: Hemlock has smooth stems with purple blotches and a musty smell, while Queen Anne's Lace has hairy stems and a carroty smell when crushed.

Jack-in-the-Pulpit *(Arisaema triphyllum)*

Looks Like: Wild Garlic *(Allium ursinum)*

Differentiating Factor: Jack-in-the-Pulpit has a distinctive hooded flower and three-part leaves, whereas Wild Garlic has grass-like leaves and a strong garlic odor.

Lily-of-the-Valley *(Convallaria majalis)*

Looks Like: Wild Garlic *(Allium ursinum)*

Differentiating Factor: Lily-of-the-Valley has smooth, broad leaves and small, bell-shaped white flowers, whereas Wild Garlic has narrower leaves and a distinct garlic smell.

Monkshood *(Aconitum napellus)*

Looks Like: Wild Geranium *(Geranium maculatum)*

Differentiating Factor: Monkshood has helmet-shaped blue or purple flowers, while Wild Geranium has five-petaled pink or purple flowers, not helmet-shaped.

Poison Hemlock *(Conium maculatum)*

Looks Like: Cow Parsnip *(Heracleum maximum)*

Differentiating Factor: Poison Hemlock has smooth, hollow stems with purple spots and finely divided leaves, while Cow Parsnip has coarse, hairy stems and larger, broader leaves.

Poison Oak *(Toxicodendron diversilobum)*

Looks Like: Blackberry *(Rubus spp.)*

Differentiating Factor: Poison Oak has three leaflets with scalloped edges and no thorns, while Blackberry has multiple leaflets with serrated edges and thorny stems.

Water Hemlock *(Cicuta maculata)*

Looks Like: Elderflower *(Sambucus nigra)*

Differentiating Factor: Water Hemlock has smooth stems with purple streaks and a strong, unpleasant odor, while Elderflower has woody stems and a pleasant, floral fragrance.

- Pine Nuts
- Porcini
- Red Clover (Trifolium pratense)
- Red Columbine
- Salmonberries
- Stinging Nettle (Urtica dioica)
- Thimbleberries
- Watercress
- Wild Carrots
- Wild Onions
- Wild Potatoes
- Wild Rose
- Yarrow (Achillea millefolium)

Conclusion

Foraging has always been a way of life. Even today, with people relying on markets and grocery stores, many still prefer living sustainably. However, foraging should be done correctly for your safety and to protect the environment. This book provides all the necessary information to get you started.

It began by introducing you to the world of foraging in the Pacific Northwest and its diverse ecosystem. You discovered its history, the region's nature, and how to identify edible plants. Collecting plants isn't a simple procedure. You must have specific tools and equipment, wear appropriate clothes, and practice safety while foraging. You should be aware of the changing weather conditions, poisonous plants, dangerous wildlife, and other challenges.

Throughout the year, nature changes its colors and brings a variety of wild edible plants, providing a unique foraging experience each season. You learned about the most common plants in the Pacific Northwest, their availability, terrain, and harvesting techniques.

Then, you explored each plant's habitats, characteristics, nutritional benefits, and seasonal nuances. Some edible and poisonous plants look alike. So, learning to identify safe plants protects you from potential hazards.

The Pacific Northwest has the ideal climate and forests for edible and medicinal mushrooms and fungi to thrive, making it perfect for foragers. The book explains mushrooms' diversity, complexity, and ecological significance. It provided information on their anatomy and terminology with tips to distinguish between edible, inedible, and poisonous mushrooms.

People forage plants and mushrooms to cook healthy and delicious meals. You discovered various recipes highlighting the unique flavors of foraged edibles.

People used medicinal flowers, mushroom greens, etc., for centuries to treat ailments. The Pacific Northwest is a paradise for these plants. You learned about the concepts of natural remedies and herbalism and the therapeutic properties of healing plants.

If you keep taking from nature, it will eventually run out of resources. Protect the environment to ensure future generations will find abundant edible plants by practicing sustainable harvesting and ethical foraging.

Although foraging will give you independence and connect you with nature, it isn't for everyone. You must ask yourself if this is the right lifestyle for you. Now it's time to visualize your life as a forager, knowing you have learned its advantages for your well-being and the environment.

Use this book's information to live a free and sustainable life in harmony with nature.

If you enjoyed this book, I'd greatly appreciate a review on Amazon because it helps me to create more books that people want. It would mean a lot to hear from you.

To leave a review:
1. Open your camera app.
2. Point your mobile device at the QR code.
3. The review page will appear in your web browser.

Thanks for your support!

Here's another book by Dion Rosser that you might like

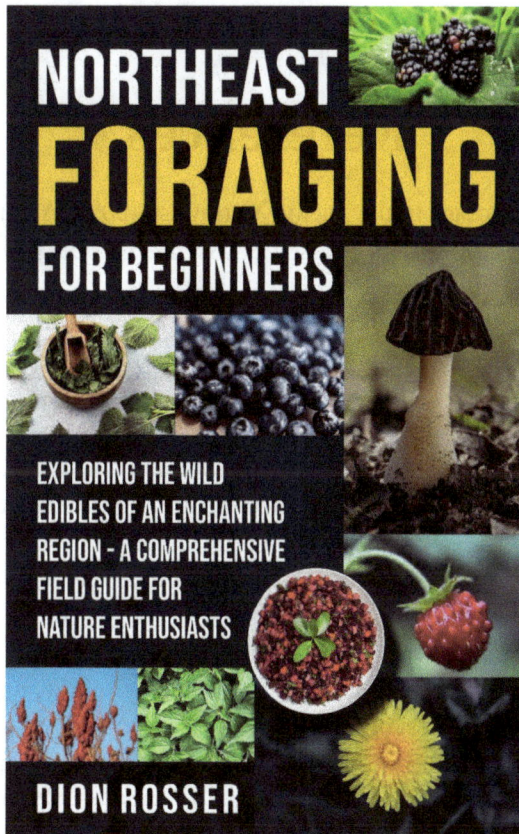

References

13 Plants You Can Forage in the Pacific Northwest. (2022, August 18). Anja Jane. https://www.anjajane.com/blogs/journal/13-plants-you-can-forage-in-the-pacific-northwest

A Beginner's Guide to Safe Wild Mushroom Foraging. (n.d.). Www.incrediblemushrooms.com. https://www.incrediblemushrooms.com/wild-mushroom-foraging.html

A LMANAC Pacific Northwest Region. (2017). https://www.fs.usda.gov/Internet/FSE_DOCUMENTS/fseprd529709.pdf

Andytofu. (n.d.). Sausage and Beef Stuffed Acorn Squash. Allrecipes. https://www.allrecipes.com/recipe/64311/stuffed-acorn-squash-ii/

Aubrey. (2022, September 4). Lobster Mushroom Recipe. Aubrey's Kitchen. https://aubreyskitchen.com/lobster-mushroom-recipe/#recipe

Better Health Channel. (2012). Herbal medicine. Better Health Channel. https://www.betterhealth.vic.gov.au/health/ConditionsAndTreatments/herbal-medicine

Bioregional Herbalism: 10 Wild and Weedy Herbs of the Pacific NW - Wildflower School of Botanical Medicine. (2019, August 12). WILDFLOWER SCHOOL of BOTANICAL MEDICINE. https://wildflowerherbschool.com/bioregional-herbalism-10-wild-and-weedy-herbs-of-the-pacific-nw/

Blankespoor, J., & Gemma, M. (2019, March 8). Essential Foraging Tools and Supplies. Chestnut School of Herbal Medicine. https://chestnutherbs.com/essential-foraging-tools-and-supplies/

Blizzard, K. (2017, April 20). Mushroom Identification + Edibility: A Systematic Approach. Modern Forager. https://modern-forager.com/mushroom-identification-edibility-systematic-approach/

Boyd, S. (2020, October 29). Foraging in the Pacific Northwest Is a Search for Hope Amid the Pandemic. Eater Seattle. https://seattle.eater.com/2020/10/29/21538918/foraging-in-the-pacific-northwest-quarantine-cooking

Buice, T. (2013, July 1). Blackberry Frozen Yogurt. Saving Room for Dessert. https://www.savingdessert.com/blackberry-frozen-yogurt/#wprm-recipe-container-18940

Cornbread, C. (2013, July 14). Homemade Fireweed Jelly from Cosmopolitan Cornbread. Cosmopolitan Cornbread. https://cosmopolitancornbread.com/fireweed-jelly-3/

Dalkin, G. (2018, June 11). Wild Mushroom Tart - What's Gaby Cooking. Whatsgabycooking.com. https://whatsgabycooking.com/wild-mushroom-tart/#recipeJump

Date and Pine Nut Smoothie. (n.d.). Www.stockland.com.au. https://www.stockland.com.au/shopping-centres/everyday-ideas/recipe/date-and-pine-nut-smoothie

Daum, A. (2020, June 15). Elderflower Lemonade. Occasionally Eggs. https://www.occasionallyeggs.com/elderflower-lemonade/#wprm-recipe-container-9126

Deurlein, R. (2023, January 20). Foraging: Good for the Body, Good for the Soul – Good Grit Magazine. Https://Goodgritmag.com/. https://goodgritmag.com/blogs/news/foraging-good-for-the-body-good-for-the-soul

Foret, X. (2012, August 8). Edible Plants of the Pacific Northwest Coast. Sustainable Living Project. https://sustainablelivingproject.blogspot.com/2012/08/edible-plants-of-pacific-northwest-coast.html

foreverintheforest. (2015, April 23). Flavours of the Pacific Northwest: Spring Foraging. Foreverintheforest. https://foreverintheforest.wordpress.com/2015/04/23/flavours-of-the-pacific-northwest-spring-foraging/

GERMANY, E. (n.d.). Dandelion Salad. Allrecipes. https://www.allrecipes.com/recipe/49713/dandelion-salad/

Glossary of useful terms. (n.d.). Fungimap. https://fungimap.org.au/about-fungi/glossary-of-useful-terms/

GRAVALESE, S. (2024, May 2). 10 Tips for Foraging with Wild Edibles. Slow Living Kitchen. https://slowlivingkitchen.com/tips-for-foraging/

Gretchen. (2019, August 15). Pizza with Chanterelles, Green Onions, Brie, Arugula, and Lemon. Three Big Bites. https://threebigbites.com/2019-8-15-pizza-with-chanterelles-green-onions-brie-arugula-and-lemon/#recipe

Gucker, C. (2012). Rubus parviflorus. Www.fs.usda.gov. https://www.fs.usda.gov/database/feis/plants/shrub/rubpar/all.html

Hafer, A. (2023, September 9). Essential Foraging Tools: 5 Must-Have Items for Successful Wild Food Harvesting. Outdoors with Bear Grylls. https://outdoors.com/essential-foraging-tools/

HISTORY OF FORAGING. (n.d.). Researchproject. https://hklang.wixsite.com/researchproject/history-of-foraging

Ingram, B. (2017, May 7). Practicing the Foraging Lifestyle. Smoky Mountain Living. https://www.smliv.com/outdoors/practicing-the-foraging-lifestyle/

Is Foraging Sustainable? (n.d.). Four Season Foraging. https://www.fourseasonforaging.com/blog/2019/1/17/is-foraging-sustainable

Jane, A. (2022, August 18). 13 Plants You Can Forage in the Pacific Northwest. Anja Jane. https://www.anjajane.com/blogs/journal/13-plants-you-can-forage-in-the-pacific-northwest

Jenny. (2024, March 18). Spring Mushroom Foraging In The Southwest - Mushroom Appreciation. Www.mushroom-Appreciation.com. https://www.mushroom-appreciation.com/spring-mushroom-foraging-in-the-southwest.html

johnsoulesfoods. (2022, September 2). Cooking Tips for Beginners. JohnSoulesFoods. https://www.johnsoulesfoods.com/blog/cooking-tips-for-beginners/

Joyce. (2022, March 24). Nettle Potato Soup (& Benefits of Nettles!). Joyjam Kitchen. https://joyjamkitchen.com/nettle-potato-soup/#recipe

Kubala, J. (2021, June 3). Foraging for Food: Tips, Common Foods, Safety, and More. Healthline. https://www.healthline.com/nutrition/foraging-for-food

Lambert, R. (2018, December 20). Foraging as a Way to Feel Connected. Wild Walks Southwest. https://www.wildwalks-southwest.co.uk/foraging-as-a-way-to-feel-connected/

Lorse, S. (2022, September 14). The Dandy Dandelion. Salish Magazine. https://salishmagazine.org/the-dandy-dandelion/

Madrian, K. (n.d.). Huckleberry Cheesecake. Allrecipes. https://www.allrecipes.com/recipe/258711/huckleberry-cheesecake/

Mihail, A. (2023, July 11). Foraging in The Modern World: Rediscovering an Ancient Practice. Www.foodunfolded.com. https://www.foodunfolded.com/article/foraging-in-the-modern-world-rediscovering-an-ancient-practice

Mushroom Anatomy: Understanding Caps + Stems. (n.d.). R&R Cultivation. https://rrcultivation.com/blogs/mn/mushroom-anatomy-caps-stems

NHS . (2022, October 18). Herbal Medicines. NHS. https://www.nhs.uk/conditions/herbal-medicines/

Nichols, M. (2023, June 4). Morel Mushroom and Herb Stuffed Chicken Recipe. Recipes.net. https://recipes.net/mushroom-recipes/morel-mushroom/morel-mushroom-and-herb-stuffed-chicken-recipe/#google_vignette

Odenwalder, A. (2022, November 1). Porcini Mushroom Lasagna - This Is How I Cook. This Is How I Cook. https://thisishowicook.com/porcini-mushroom-lasagna/#tasty-recipes-21188-jump-target

Palmer, R. (2021, July 4). 10 Reasons Why Foraging Is Good For You * Marvellous Mrs P - Lifestyle, Vintage & Family Blog. Marvellous Mrs P - Lifestyle, Vintage & Family Blog. https://www.marvellousmrsp.com/10-reasons-why-foraging-is-good-for-you/

Patterson, M. (n.d.). The Edible and Medicinal Plants of the Pacific Northwest · iNaturalist. INaturalist. https://www.inaturalist.org/guides/10285

Professionals, P. I. for H. (2021, February 20). What Herbalism is and Why It's Important Today. Climb.pcc.edu. https://climb.pcc.edu/blog/what-herbalism-is-and-why-its-important-today

Raspberry Sorbet | Sorbet Recipes. (n.d.). Tesco Real Food. https://realfood.tesco.com/recipes/raspberry-sorbet.html

Sandberg, A. (2015, January 28). Hazelnut-Crusted Salmon. Completely Delicious. https://www.completelydelicious.com/hazelnut-crusted-salmon/#recipe

Shannon. (2018, June 18). Spring Foraging in the PNW. HONEST MAGAZINE. https://www.honestquarterly.com/blog/spring-foraging

Shaw, H. (2017a, August 3). Chanterelle mushroom risotto. Hunter Angler Gardener Cook. https://honest-food.net/chanterelle-risotto-recipe/#wprm-recipe-container-25012

Spring Foraging in the PNW. (2018, June 18). HONEST MAGAZINE. https://www.honestquarterly.com/blog/spring-foraging

Steele, Marjorie. (2023, November 6). Forget Digital: the Future is Foraging. Medium. https://creativeonion.medium.com/forget-digital-the-future-is-foraging-4006f38c7ea1

The Joys of Foraging. (n.d.). Www.squaremilefarms.com. https://www.squaremilefarms.com/post/the-joys-of-foraging

Tools and Resources for the Modern Forager. (n.d.). Modern Forager. https://modern-forager.com/resources/

tovlakas. (2020, June 18). Blackberry Puff Pastry Tarts. Allrecipes. https://www.allrecipes.com/recipe/137839/blackberry-puff-pastry-tarts/

University of Rochester Medical Center. (2014). A Guide to Common Medicinal Herbs - Health Encyclopedia - University of Rochester Medical Center. Rochester.edu; University of Rochester Medical Center. https://www.urmc.rochester.edu/encyclopedia/content.aspx?contenttypeid=1&contentid=1169

urbanforageur. (2012, January 9). Winter Foraging in the Pacific Northwest. Urbanforageur. https://urbanforageur.wordpress.com/2012/01/09/winter-foraging-in-the-pacific-northwest/

Watercress, avocado & lime smoothie. (2018, August 15). Watercress | Health, Recipes & More. https://www.watercress.co.uk/blog/2018/8/15/watercress-avocado-lime-smoothie?rq=avocado

Wild Edible Plants of the Pacific Northwest. (n.d.). Www.northernbushcraft.com. https://www.northernbushcraft.com/plants/

Yates, T. (n.d.). Climate and Weather along the Pacific Northwest National Scenic Trail. PNT. https://www.pnt.org/pnta/know-before-you-go/plan-your-trip/climate-weather/

Image Sources

[1] https://www.pexels.com/photo/rough-cliff-by-sea-21815243/

[2] https://www.pexels.com/photo/person-holding-fruit-on-plant-704756/

[3] https://www.pexels.com/photo/black-ring-in-front-of-white-orchid-selective-focus-photography-979933/

[4] https://www.pexels.com/photo/silhouette-of-man-at-daytime-1051838/

[5] https://www.pexels.com/photo/a-person-s-hand-near-brown-grass-6056165/

[6] https://www.pexels.com/photo/gray-and-black-folding-pocket-knife-168804/

[7] https://www.pexels.com/photo/a-person-using-pruning-shears-12142540/

[8] https://unsplash.com/photos/beige-sling-bag-s6M63HPGb5E

[9] https://unsplash.com/photos/opened-flower-book-on-table-GQauWfILQiw

[10] https://www.pexels.com/search/first%20aid%20kit/

[11] https://www.pexels.com/photo/foods-stored-on-zip-lock-bags-10361128/

[12] Jason Hollinger, CC BY 2.0 <https://creativecommons.org/licenses/by/2.0>, via Wikimedia Commons: https://commons.wikimedia.org/wiki/File:False_Morel.jpg

[13] https://commons.wikimedia.org/wiki/File:Magnifying_Glass_Photo.jpg

[14] https://www.pexels.com/photo/food-inside-green-food-containers-on-purple-surface-5971998/

[15] https://www.pexels.com/photo/round-grey-and-black-compass-1736222/

[16] https://pixabay.com/photos/ipad-map-tablet-internet-screen-632394/

[17] PumpkinSky, CC BY-SA 4.0 <https://creativecommons.org/licenses/by-sa/4.0>, via Wikimedia Commons https://commons.wikimedia.org/wiki/File:Work_glove_for_right_hand_LR.jpg

[18] https://unsplash.com/photos/brown-leaves-on-brown-wooden-plank-LIcAPq4Ldx4

[19] https://pixabay.com/photos/tulips-daffodils-flowers-field-1197602/

[20] *https://pixabay.com/photos/thermometer-summer-hot-heat-sun-3581190/*

[21] *https://pixabay.com/photos/leaves-foliage-maple-tree-branches-507544/*

[22] *https://pixabay.com/photos/winter-trees-snow-winter-landscape-8435314/*

[23] *H. Zell, CC BY-SA 3.0 <https://creativecommons.org/licenses/by-sa/3.0>, via Wikimedia Commons: https://commons.wikimedia.org/wiki/File:Taraxacum_officinale_001.JPG*

[24] *Stefan Lefnaer, CC BY-SA 4.0 <https://creativecommons.org/licenses/by-sa/4.0>, via Wikimedia Commons. https://commons.wikimedia.org/wiki/File:Hypochaeris_radicata_sl3.jpg*

[25] *Rob Hille, CC BY-SA 3.0 <https://creativecommons.org/licenses/by-sa/3.0>, via Wikimedia Commons: https://commons.wikimedia.org/wiki/File:Claytonia_perfoliata_R.H_(3).JPG*

[26] *Hugo.arg, CC BY-SA 4.0 <https://creativecommons.org/licenses/by-sa/4.0>, via Wikimedia Commons: https://commons.wikimedia.org/wiki/File:ChenopodiumAlbum001.JPG*

[27] *Stefan Lefnaer, CC BY-SA 4.0 <https://creativecommons.org/licenses/by-sa/4.0>, via Wikimedia Commons: https://commons.wikimedia.org/wiki/File:Nasturtium_officinale_(s._str.)_sl18.jpg*

[28] *Otto Sheva2, CC BY-SA 4.0 <https://creativecommons.org/licenses/by-sa/4.0>, via Wikimedia Commons: https://commons.wikimedia.org/wiki/File:Sambucus-nigra_foliage.jpg*

[29] *Nicolas Ramirez, CC BY-SA 4.0 <https://creativecommons.org/licenses/by-sa/4.0>, via Wikimedia Commons. https://commons.wikimedia.org/wiki/File:Conium_maculatum_007.jpg*

[30] *Zeynel Cebeci, CC BY-SA 4.0 <https://creativecommons.org/licenses/by-sa/4.0>, via Wikimedia Commons: https://commons.wikimedia.org/wiki/File:Chamerion_angustifolium_(Epilobium_angustifolium)-_Fireweed_-_Yak%C4%B1otu_4.jpg*

[31] *Walter Siegmund, CC BY-SA 3.0 <https://creativecommons.org/licenses/by-sa/3.0>, via Wikimedia Commons: https://upload.wikimedia.org/wikipedia/commons/f/fb/Rosa_nutkana_with_sepals.JPG*

[32] *Татьяна Прозорова, CC0, via Wikimedia Commons: https://commons.wikimedia.org/wiki/File:Vaccinium_myrtillus_30999834.jpg*

[33] *Apv at en.Wikipedia, CC BY 2.5 <https://creativecommons.org/licenses/by/2.5>, via Wikimedia Commons: https://commons.wikimedia.org/wiki/File:Red-salmonberry.jpg*

[34] *Walter Siegmund, CC BY-SA 3.0 <https://creativecommons.org/licenses/by-sa/3.0>, via Wikimedia Commons: https://commons.wikimedia.org/wiki/File:Rubus_parviflorus_9481.JPG*

[35] *H. Zell, CC BY-SA 3.0 <https://creativecommons.org/licenses/by-sa/3.0>, via Wikimedia Commons: https://commons.wikimedia.org/wiki/File:Rubus_fruticosus_003.JPG*

[36] *© Hans Hillewaert: https://commons.wikimedia.org/wiki/File:Quercus_coccifera_(acorn).jpg*

[37] *Superior National Forest, CC BY 2.0 <https://creativecommons.org/licenses/by/2.0>, via Wikimedia Commons https://commons.wikimedia.org/wiki/File:Corylus_cornuta_fruit_(5097503079).jpg*

[38] *Dominicus Johannes Bergsma, CC BY-SA 4.0 <https://creativecommons.org/licenses/by-sa/4.0>, via Wikimedia Commons. https://commons.wikimedia.org/wiki/File:Gebarsten_bolster_van_een_paardenkastanje_(Aesculus)_20-09-2020_(d.j.b.)_01.jpg*

[39] Gmihail at Serbian Wikipedia, CC BY-SA 3.0 RS <https://creativecommons.org/licenses/by-sa/3.0/rs/deed.en>, via Wikimedia Commons: https://commons.wikimedia.org/wiki/File:Juglans_nigra_nuts.jpg

[40] https://commons.wikimedia.org/wiki/File:Camassia_quamash_2_FR_2013.jpg

[41] https://commons.wikimedia.org/wiki/File:Toxicoscordion_venenosum_-_Craig_Martin_01.jpg

[42] Christian Fischer, CC BY-SA 3.0 <https://creativecommons.org/licenses/by-sa/3.0>, via Wikimedia Commons: https://commons.wikimedia.org/wiki/File:ArctiumLappa1.jpg

[43] Kor!An (Андрей Корзун), CC BY-SA 3.0 <https://creativecommons.org/licenses/by-sa/3.0>, via Wikimedia Commons: https://commons.wikimedia.org/wiki/File:Allium_sp._03.JPG

[44] Krzysztof Ziarnek, CC BY-SA 3.0 <http://creativecommons.org/licenses/by-sa/3.0/>, via Wikimedia Commons: https://commons.wikimedia.org/wiki/File:Daucus_carota_inflorescence_kz.jpg

[45] Magnefl, CC BY-SA 4.0 <https://creativecommons.org/licenses/by-sa/4.0>, via Wikimedia Commons. https://commons.wikimedia.org/wiki/File:Conium_maculatum_blad.jpg

[46] https://pixabay.com/photos/mushrooms-beautiful-bonnet-wood-3647871/

[47] Zhousun21, CC0, via Wikimedia Commons: https://commons.wikimedia.org/wiki/File:Parts_of_a_mushroom.jpg

[48] https://pixabay.com/photos/fungus-mushroom-sponge-basket-1194380/

[49] https://commons.wikimedia.org/wiki/File:Amanita_phalloides_2011_G3.jpg

[50] Eli T. (mythical_mold), CC BY 4.0 <https://creativecommons.org/licenses/by/4.0>, via Wikimedia Commons. https://commons.wikimedia.org/wiki/File:Amanita_bisporigera_destroying_angel_skirt.jpg

[51] John.Chy, Copyrighted free use, via Wikimedia Commons. https://commons.wikimedia.org/wiki/File:Omphalotus_olearius_in_NE_IL.JPG

[52] Andreas Kunze, CC BY-SA 3.0 <https://creativecommons.org/licenses/by-sa/3.0>, via Wikimedia Commons: https://commons.wikimedia.org/wiki/File:2007-07-14_Cantharellus_cibarius.jpg

[53] This image was created by user Ron Pastorino (Ronpast) at Mushroom Observer, a source for mycological images. CC BY-SA 3.0 <https://creativecommons.org/licenses/by-sa/3.0>, via Wikimedia Commons: https://commons.wikimedia.org/wiki/File:2011-05-06_Morchella_frustrata_M.Kuo_145786.jpg

[54] This image was created by user Dan Molter (shroomydan) at Mushroom Observer, a source for mycological images. CC BY-SA 3.0 <https://creativecommons.org/licenses/by-sa/3.0>, via Wikimedia Commons: https://commons.wikimedia.org/wiki/File:Hypomyces_lactifluorum_169126.jpg

[55] Henk Monster, CC BY 3.0 <https://creativecommons.org/licenses/by/3.0>, via Wikimedia Commons: https://commons.wikimedia.org/wiki/File:Pleurotus_ostreatus_(Oyster_Mushroom,_D%3D_Austernseitling,_F%3D_Pleurote_en_forme_d%27hu%C3%AEtre_ou_P._en_coquille,_NL%3D_Gewone_oesterzwam)_white_spores_and_causes_white_rot,_near_Watermuseum_Arnhem_-_panoramio.jpg

[56] This image was created by user Richard Sullivan (enchplant) at Mushroom Observer, a source for mycological images. CC BY-SA 3.0 <https://creativecommons.org/licenses/by-sa/3.0>, via Wikimedia Commons: https://commons.wikimedia.org/wiki/File:Hericium_erinaceus_64176_02.jpg

[57] Strobilomyces, CC BY-SA 4.0 <https://creativecommons.org/licenses/by-sa/4.0>, via Wikimedia Commons: https://commons.wikimedia.org/wiki/File:Boletus_edulis_EtgHollande_041031_091.jpg

[58] Japonica, CC BY-SA 4.0 <https://creativecommons.org/licenses/by-sa/4.0>, via Wikimedia Commons. https://commons.wikimedia.org/wiki/File:Tricholoma_matsutake_1988_11_Saizaki_Japan.jpg

[59] James Lindsey at Ecology of Commanster, CC BY-SA 2.5 <https://creativecommons.org/licenses/by-sa/2.5>, via Wikimedia Commons: https://commons.wikimedia.org/wiki/File:Sparassis.crispa.-.lindsey.jpg

[60] This image was created by user Huafang at Mushroom Observer, a source for mycological images. CC BY-SA 3.0 <https://creativecommons.org/licenses/by-sa/3.0>, via Wikimedia Commons: https://commons.wikimedia.org/wiki/File:Laetiporus_sulphureus_(850755).jpg

[61] Katrin Gilger, CC BY-SA 2.0 <https://creativecommons.org/licenses/by-sa/2.0>, via Wikimedia Commons: https://commons.wikimedia.org/wiki/File:Mushroom_Risotto_(4790048714).jpg

[62] https://www.pexels.com/photo/a-close-up-shot-of-a-scooped-ice-cream-5535557/

[63] https://www.pexels.com/photo/leek-and-potato-soup-5794/

[64] Jessica Spengler, CC BY 2.0 <https://creativecommons.org/licenses/by/2.0>, via Wikimedia Commons: https://commons.wikimedia.org/wiki/File:Mini_mushroom_and_cheddar_quiches,_2007.jpg

[65] T.Tseng, CC BY 2.0 <https://creativecommons.org/licenses/by/2.0>, via Wikimedia Commons: https://commons.wikimedia.org/wiki/File:Hinbe,_dandelion_greens,_lemon,_garlic,_fried_shallots.jpg

[66] Morgan "Mogsy" Daniel, CC BY-SA 4.0 <https://creativecommons.org/licenses/by-sa/4.0>, via Wikimedia Commons: https://commons.wikimedia.org/wiki/File:A_pot_of_strawberry_jelly.jpg

[67] Bing, CC BY 2.0 <https://creativecommons.org/licenses/by/2.0>, via Wikimedia Commons: https://commons.wikimedia.org/wiki/File:Blackberry_currant_and_sweet_apple_tart_at_Clear_Flour_Bread_Bakery.jpg

[68] Bawani Sri Jayaveeran, CC BY-SA 4.0 <https://creativecommons.org/licenses/by-sa/4.0>, via Wikimedia Commons: https://commons.wikimedia.org/wiki/File:Malaysian_Stir_Fry_Glass_Noodle.jpg

[69] https://pixabay.com/photos/green-smoothie-juice-mixed-drink-1066168/

[70] https://pixabay.com/photos/garlic-fresh-garlic-garlic-capsules-4830671/

[71] The original uploader was Meggar at English Wikipedia., CC BY-SA 3.0 <http://creativecommons.org/licenses/by-sa/3.0/>, via Wikimedia Commons: https://commons.wikimedia.org/wiki/File:Mahonia_aquifolium.jpg

[72] *H. Zell, CC BY-SA 3.0 <https://creativecommons.org/licenses/by-sa/3.0>, via Wikimedia Commons: https://commons.wikimedia.org/wiki/File:Trifolium_pratense_002.JPG*

[73] *Petar Milošević, CC BY-SA 4.0 <https://creativecommons.org/licenses/by-sa/4.0>, via Wikimedia Commons: https://commons.wikimedia.org/wiki/File:Yarrow_(Achillea_millefolium).jpg*

[74] *H. Zell, CC BY-SA 3.0 <https://creativecommons.org/licenses/by-sa/3.0>, via Wikimedia Commons: https://commons.wikimedia.org/wiki/File:Echinacea_purpurea_001.JPG*

[75] *Jesse Taylor, CC BY-SA 3.0 <https://creativecommons.org/licenses/by-sa/3.0>, via Wikimedia Commons: https://commons.wikimedia.org/wiki/File:Rhamnus_purshiana_--_leaves_and_fruits.JPG*

[76] *Dinnye, CC BY-SA 3.0 <https://creativecommons.org/licenses/by-sa/3.0>, via Wikimedia Commons: https://commons.wikimedia.org/wiki/File:Flowers_of_Mentha_%C3%97_piperita.jpg*

[77] *Norbert Nagel, Mörfelden-Walldorf, Germany, CC BY-SA 3.0 <https://creativecommons.org/licenses/by-sa/3.0>, via Wikimedia Commons: https://commons.wikimedia.org/wiki/File:Stinging_nettle_-_Gro%C3%9Fe_Brennnessel_-_Urtica_dioica_03.jpg*

[78] *https://pixabay.com/photos/chinese-medicine-fill-a-prescription-3666268/*

[79] *https://pixabay.com/photos/city-road-traffic-footbridge-cars-6645646/*

[80] *https://unsplash.com/photos/maple-leaf-illustration-c0rIh0nFTFU*

[81] *https://unsplash.com/photos/woman-sitting-on-bench-over-viewing-mountain-HS5CLnQbCOc*

www.ingramcontent.com/pod-product-compliance
Lightning Source LLC
Chambersburg PA
CBHW070757300326
41914CB00053B/717